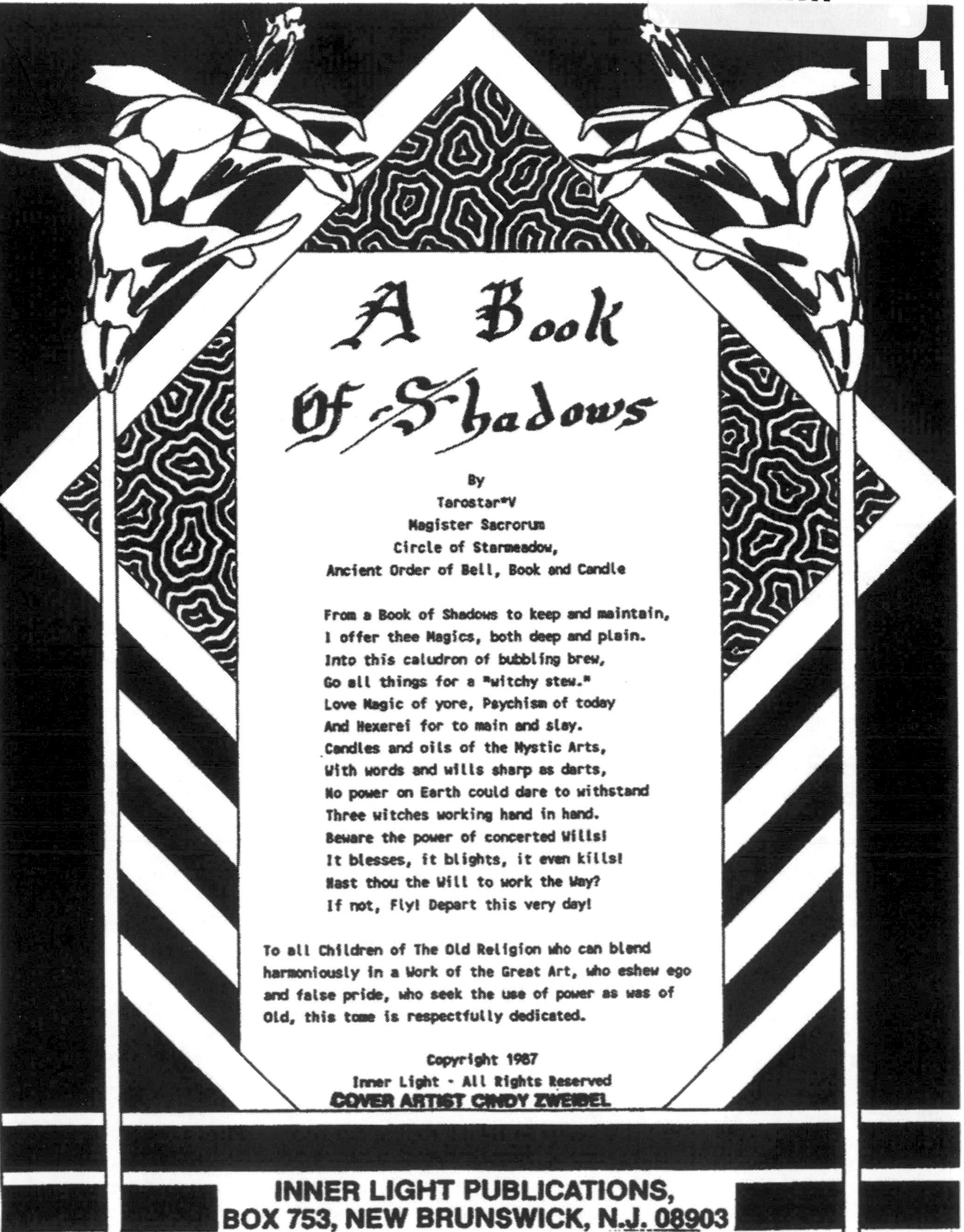
A Book
Of Shadows
By
Tarostar*V
Magister Sacrorum
Circle of Starmeadow,
Ancient Order of Bell, Book and Candle
From a Book of Shadows to keep and maintain,
I offer thee Magics, both deep and plain.
Into this caludron of bubbling brew,
Go all things for a "witchy stew."
Love Magic of yore, Psychism of today
And Hexerei for to main and slay.
Candles and oils of the Mystic Arts,
With words and wills sharp as darts,
No power on Earth could dare to withstand
Three witches working hand in hand.
Beware the power of concerted Wills!
It blesses, it blights, it even kills!
Hast thou the Will to work the Way?
If not, Fly! Depart this very day!
To all Children of The Old Religion who can blend harmoniously in a Work of the Great Art, who eshew ego and false pride, who seek the use of power as was of Old, this tome is respectfully dedicated.
Copyright 1987
Inner Light - All Rights Reserved
COVER ARTIST CINDY ZWEIBEL
INNER LIGHT PUBLICATIONS,
BOX 753, NEW BRUNSWICK, N.J. 08903

CONTENTS

PART ONE

PART TWO

BLESSED BE TO ALL

Ring the Bell, light the candle and open the Book of Shadows..... has long been the gesture of seeking arcane lore and delving into the mysterious Powers that rule the Universe. Wizards, Witches, Magicians and Students of The Occult Arts and Psychic Sciences have long sought out the Wisdom of the Ancients, found in pages of dusty and neglected tomes of hidden and forgotten knowledge.

What has been called, in recent times, the Book of Shadows, was, in previous Ages, nothing more than the personal journal of each and every literate Witch or Wizard. It was the record of personal works of Magic, both successful and unsuccessful. It also recorded the psychic and occult experiences of the one who kept such a journal.

It really never was a Liturgy Book for the practice of Witchcraft, although some have suggested such an idea in the present era.

Being a chronology of the Magical Life of its author, it would be kept by hand as a Diary and would grow and expand with time and his/her experience in the Occult.

It would be consulted as and when an occurrence presented itself, where the Practitioner needed insight into occult experiences that had gone before.

It would also be a collection, or Grimoire, if you will, of the types of Magical and/or Mystical Practices the Writer found to be useful and correct. A personal Spellbook, in other words.

Some types of books called Liber Spirituum have been proclaimed to be a Book of Shadows, but are just what the name implies: A Book of Spirits, for the conjuration of entities from other dimensions, not true Magical Journals at all.

A Book of Shadows is the record of the growth and development of the Power, in the Occult, of an individual, using his/her own forces of invoking and *evoking* energy with which to apply to matters needing metaphysical solutions.

Due to the ravages of the Witchcraft Mania, brought on by misguided Ecclesiastical fervor, due to the natural processes of decay, and due to disregard of the old lore, very few of these true Magical Journals have survived Time and come down to Modern Day.

However, many are still being written and kept by Occultists for their own use. They rarely are seen by outsiders.

Generally, they would appear to be no more than a collection of personal scribblings, of no interest to any but another Occultist. Therefore, many simply are consigned to the dump or incinerator when an Occultist passes on and his/her family clear out his/her belongings.

Unless the individual was well-known, as a Writer and/or Occult Magician, and the family members appreciated that fact, little, if any, of his/her records would survive.

More is the pity, because much personal gleanings from the Occult Study does not get into print to serve as a guideline to others who may be traveling the same line of thought.

As one begins to become actively interested in Metaphysics and the Occult, he/she should start the keeping of a journal and preservation of notes and ideas. The situations one encounters in study, practice and application of esoteric things ought to be set down, so the practical experiences are remembered and may be of benefit to the Practitioner, later in life, or to those who come after.

Blank Books, recorded in the Practitioner's own hand, is the age old traditional method used.

It does not need daily entries, but the results of Spells and Ritual Works, situations involving Occult Practices and personal observations and thoughts concerning Psychic Happenings and group or singular activity in the Ars Magica et Mystica.

In this way an authentic Book of Shadows is maintained by the true devotees of Occultism. Much lore will then not be lost.

SPACE FOR YOUR NOTES/SPELLS/RITUALS FOR YOUR PERSONAL BOOK OF SHADOWS

In previous centuries, it has been said to have been the custom to burn the writings of Wizards and Witches when they passed on. In those days it would have been dangerous for the surviving family to have been found with such things. Today, however, that is not the case.

These record books can and ought to be passed on to a Practitioner's favorite Students, or to his/her Coven to be kept as reference.

It behooves us to see that as much Occult Lore is preserved as is possible, in order to prevent a dearth of such knowledge as did result after the "Burning Time." Also, the trend to computerize the World onto tapes, discs and chips would leave out the esoteric "Soul" of the Human Race. The Ancient Wisdom must be preserved for the day when machines show their decided limitations, not being able to display a Spirit, and Humanity will need most the esoteric Wisdom of Yore.

For this reason alone, each Student of the Occult Arts and Psychic Sciences should begin and faithfully keep a Book of Shadows.

THE MIND IS THE CRUCIBLE OF MAGIC

Let us first define the term. What is Magic? The best definition so far brought forward by the myriad of writers on this theme is: THE ART OF CAUSING CHANGES TO OCCUR IN SITUATIONS, IN CONFORMITY TO YOUR WILL.

That understanding of the word Magic brings it down to the Human level of application. One may will that a Leopard change his spots, but such a Will could never buck Dame Nature. One can, however, will that certain other people do things, or take specific courses of action, and can, by magical methods, bring such about.

There is mystery and wonder, magic, if you will, in the unfolding of a flower bud. that type of Magic does not depend on a Human Will.

Manipulative Magic is the work of the Human Will, as a Species.

A Will built the Suez Canal, wrapped islands with pink plastic, erected the Sears Tower, etc.

It did so by the application of Principles.

It is the application of Metaphysical Principles which will work the mystery we call Magic.

You must produce an emotional vibration, give it intention, or "charge" it, as was said of old, and direct it by force and Will.

You must produce an emotional vibration, give it intention, or "charge" it, as was said of old, and direct it by force of Will.

IMAGINATION, WILL, and FAITH, the operations of which, kept secret, produces Power from the Practitioner's own mind.

You should develop the ability of a single pointed concentration and the knack of conjuring and controlling visions in the imagination. The more emotional feeling the visions are able to arouse in you, the more potent they will be in casting Spells and working Magic.

Your Will is the focusing lens through which emotionally charged vibrations pour forth from you into the atmosphere around about.

Hold steady to your faith in yourself and your ability in working Magic. Picture your intentions as happening and act as if the desire is in the process of coming about.

Keep the workings of your Magic secret from the Multitude, the Crass and the Vulgar.

You use the electrical elements which flow through your own mind; id est, your own emotions and desires.

The materials and objects you use in a Spell are not magical per se. The effect they have as "symbols" in your own Subconscious, to stimulate emotional excitement and conjure the desired intention to your Mind's Eye, however, is magical.

In this respect there is no difference in what is called White or Black Magic. The power conjured and directed is in itself neutral. The only difference at all is in the intention of the one working with it. The personal "ethics" of the Practitioner, in other words.

Take heed, my pet! Mental doubts cause Magic to fail. Never give in to doubt. Never try to reason it out. Magic is an emotional

SPACE FOR YOUR NOTES/SPELLS/RITUALS FOR YOUR PERSONAL BOOK OF SHADOWS

Art, not a rational one. Once you doubt, all your works come to naught.

THE ARTS OF VENUS

Love Magic does not work by invoking any Powers or Potencies outside the Practitioner him/herself. It works through a gentle, romantic nature of a feeling *evoked* from inside.

The old way of working was to call upon the name of one of the Ancient Goddesses of Love to lend power to one's Spells. However, today it is sufficient to work only under the influence of the correct Astrological Time and Lunar Phase.

Friday is the usual Day or Night of Venus and the Waxing Moon most often used to start, foster or strengthen Spells designed for affairs of the heart.

The influences of Monday for Luna and Tuesday for Mars are the lesser times to cast Love Magics, and sometimes the Waning Moon can be used for binding and punishing faithless Lovers.

Individual Gods and Goddesses were from more unenlightened times and not very effective in the Modern World. *They may be used as symbols to evoke from inside.*

The Father/Mother which created and sustains the Universe simply established Laws of Spirit and Laws of Matter with the *Grey Area* in between, where Magic can work.

That grey area was and is called the Etheric or Astral Plane by those knowledgeable in Psychism or Spiritualism. Do not waste time trying to speculate on it, simply use it as you feel best for Spells and Magics. It is the art of causing vibrations and resonating them onto the grey area which will help bring success in Spellcasting.

Sweet scented Incenses, floral Oils, Herbs and Candles, etc., all help the mind steam itself up to produce the correct vibration.

Then, during the casting of the Spell itself, rhythm is used to induce the emotional state in the operator, conducive for it.

Reiteration of a rhythmic chant embodying the "idea" of a Spell over and over again, for a good twenty minutes and repeated over several days will make things most efficacious in Magic.

One must cause the part of the Universe around one to hum, or vibrate in sympathy to the sonics which encompass the charged idea for a Spell.

Before a working is begun a few minutes pause in meditation should be taken on the Astrological Force which governs the intention for a Spell. This will link the mind with it and draw its potency to help aid the Practitioner's own energy.

That act of meditation was the long-winded invocations to the Gods in Ancient Times. However, it need not concern us overly much today. When the mental and emotional hookup has been felt to have been made, proceed with the meat of the casting.

***

21 HERB AND ROOT RITUAL CANDLE

The Arts of Venus are not exclusively for Romance and Love Relationships. They can also be employed for all purposes which lend beauty, harmony, well-being and friendly good company.

This is an All-Purpose Candle which is burned an hour each day as one specific idea along these lines is meditated upon.

Basically a White Jumbo Candle would be used, but other more specific colors can be chosen, such as pink for love, green for financial change, blue for peace, yellow for luck, etc.

On a Day or Night of Venus, as the Moon waxes, grind in a mortar and pestle a pinch or two of the following herbs and roots:

All Spice	Dandelion
Angelica Root	Dill Seed
Anise Seed	Ginger Root
Basil	Lavender
Beth Root	Lemon Verbena
Chamomile	Licorice Root
Cinnamon	Marigold
Coriander	Mugwort

SPACE FOR YOUR NOTES/SPELLS/RITUALS FOR YOUR PERSONAL BOOK OF SHADOWS

Cumin Orris Root Pwdr
Damiana Rosemary
Yarrow

Grind all well to powder.

Mix Corn Starch with water to form a paste and rub that well over the candle.

Sprinkle the powdered herbs and roots over the sticky surface of the candle and set it aside to dry.

When the paste has dried, you may anoint the candle with an Occult Oil, dressing it and dedicating it to the purpose for which it is to be burned.

As the oil is anointed onto the candle shaft, vision the benefit or boon you would attract into your life, for a good five minutes.

Then light the candle to burn for an hour as you concentrate on that idea as having already begun to manifest for you.

After the hour, snuff out the flame and put all worry and concern about the problem out of your head for 24 hours.

The next day, at the same time, repeat the candle meditation. Continue thus until the candle burns itself out, an hour each day.

According to tradition, the good things you are seeking will begin to come to you in a positive manner.

The 21 Herb and Root Ritual Candle has been handed down from the Old New Orleans Tradition in the Craft and has been successfully used by Practitioners of these Arts over the years.

***

RITUAL TO MAKE A POPPET*

Cut out a pattern such as the one shown, on hard construction paper. Trace around the pattern two times on a yard of red or pink cloth, making both the front and back of the doll. Cut them out.

The two sides are lined up and sewn together, leaving an open space at the head to stuff the doll, which will be sewn up later.

On a Night of Venus, under a Waxing Moon, anoint a red or pink candle with a Love Oil of Rose or Jasmine.

Light it to burn along with Sandalwood or Rose Incense. WORK ONLY BY THE LIGHT OF THIS CANDLE.

Cut out and stitch up the doll, chanting the name of the person the Poppet is to represent, over and over as you work and stitch.

Use red or pink thread of silk or cotton.

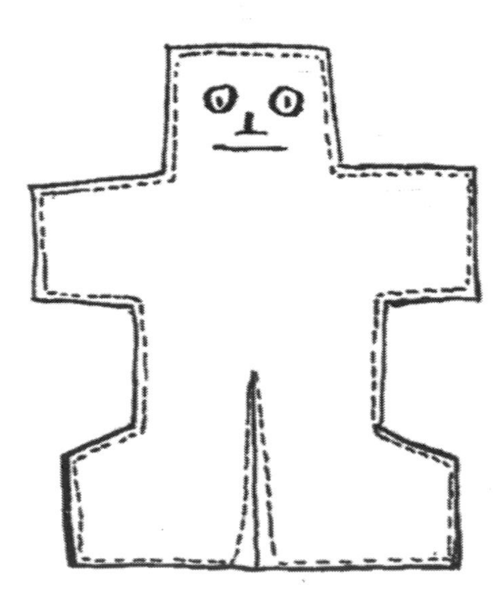

* Poppet is the customary old name given to an image doll.

SPACE FOR YOUR NOTES/SPELLS/RITUALS FOR YOUR PERSONAL BOOK OF SHADOWS

Gather together a good amount of these seven herbs:
CLOVES, for the force to compel;
ROSE BUDS, for communication between Lovers;
JASMINE, for joy in Love;
LAVENDER, for contentment in love;
DILL SEED, to make one irresistible;
APPLE BLOSSOM, to be erotic;
PEPPERMINT, for "Fast Action."

Mix the herbs thoroughly and use them to stuff the Poppet. Sew up the remaining space to seal the doll.

Stitch eyes and a mouth onto the face of the doll, best if you use thread or buttons for the eyes of the color of the person.

Stitch also a strip of parchment onto the back of the Poppet on which you have written the person's name and birth date, or the date upon which the two of you first met.

Pass the completed Poppet seven times over the flame of the candle and seven times through the incense smoke as you name it to be, in your mind, the person upon whom you will work.

Wrap it up and put it away out of sight until you have a need to use it in a Spell. Let the candle and Incense burn themselves out.

This process can be followed to make Poppets for many other purposes, such as healings, money Spells and hexes.

For a **Healing** doll, use orange or gold cloth, orange candle, Frankincense to burn and Marigold and Sunflower Petals to stuff.

For **Money**, use yellow or green candle, Mace or Cinnamon Incense, yellow or gold cloth and Dill, Cinquefoil and Sage to stuff.

For **Hexes**, use black candle, Black Arts Incense, black cloth and herbs such as Rue, Patchouli and Mullein.

The Astrological Forces would be Sun, under Waxing Moon; Mercury under Waxing Moon; Saturn under Waning Moon, respectively.

TWO POPPETS LOVE SPELL

On a Night of Venus, as the Moon waxes in a Water or Earth Sign, using the preceding format, make two Poppets, one to represent your intended Lover and one to represent yourself.

Having followed the format, you should have a properly anointed candle and a Love Incense already burning.

Still the mind and stare intently at the dolls laid before you. Untwine a length of red or pink ribbon and vision a binding power drawing the two of you together.

Chant the following:

POPPETS OF LOVE, HERBS OF DELIGHT
WORK THIS MAGIC BY CANDLELIGHT.
BIND__________TIGHT TO __________
IN LOVE FOREVER, TO PART NEVER!

Begin to twine and tie the ribbon around and around the two poppets set face to face.

Seal them together with seven knots for Venus. Hold them to your heart.

Chant, as the candle and incense burn themselves low and out:

LOVERS ENTWINED BY DAY AND NIGHT!
LETTING THEIR HEARTS TAKE UPWARD FLIGHT!
ALL THE JOYS OF LIFE AND LOVE
SHINE ON THESE TWO FROM ABOVE.

When the candle has gone out, wrap the bound Poppets in a clean cloth of their same color and hide them away in your linen drawer or closet.

When the magic has worked, and the two lovers are together, place the bound dolls to rest near the bed they share.

***

A VERY BASIC AND SIMPLE LOVE SPELL

1 Jumbo sized Red, Pink or Green Candle.
1 Bottle Orange Blossom, Rose, Jasmine or Lotus Oil.
1 Packet Love Drawing Incense, either Sandalwood or Jasmine.
1 Large pin with a red, pink or green head.

SPACE FOR YOUR NOTES/SPELLS/RITUALS FOR YOUR PERSONAL BOOK OF SHADOWS

On a Night of Venus, as the Moon waxes, with a blade, carve the name of the one you would love onto the shaft of the candle.

Anoint the candle with the oil as you chant the person's name over and over, for five minutes.

See the candle as that person, in your inner vision.

Light the incense to burn and say:

POWERS OF LOVE, COME TO THIS INCENSE.
FILL THIS ROOM WITH YOUR PRESENCE DENSE.

Drive the pin into the candle shaft in the area that would be the heart, if it were a person. Say:

'TIS LOVE I CALL TO BLESS MY LIFE.
MAKE________AND ________MAN AND WIFE!
LET NO PERSON, THING OR TIME
UNDO THE WORK I SET TO RHYME.
_________, THOU ART THE LOVER I TRULY DESIRE,
I SEE THY FACE IN THIS CANDLE FIRE!

Light the candle to burn as you vision the lover and call his/her name over and over for 1/2 hour.

Put out the candle.

Repeat the burning each night thereafter until the candle is gone.

***

NINE LOVE CANDLES AND ONE POPPET

9 Red Candles
1 Handmade Poppet, Red
1 Length of Red Ribbon or Cord
1 Bottle of Lovers Oil
1 Packet Love Drawing Incense
1 Packet Red Rose Buds & Petals
1 Piece of Parchment Paper

On a Night of Venus, as the Moon waxes, anoint each candle and your own brow with the oil.

Place them to stand in a circle around the Poppet.

Scribe the Lover's name on the piece of Parchment and wrap the doll with it and bind tight with the ribbon into seven knots.

Light the Incense and light each candle with a fresh match each, moving widdershins (Counter-clockwise) around the Circle.

Hold the doll firmly in both hands and say:

POWER OF VENUS, ON THIS NIGHT OF LOVE,
SEND MY THOUGHTS TO________ON THE WINGS OF A DOVE.
BIND THE LOVE OF MY LIFE TO BE BY MY SIDE,
THOUGH ALL THE YEARS, COME WHATEVER MAY BETIDE!

Place the doll to rest within the circle of candles.

Sprinkle the Rose Buds and Petals over it and around the formation of candles.

Allow all to burn for 1/2 hour as you vision the lover being yours.

Put the candles out and repeat the work again the next night and the next until seven nights have passed.

Toss all the left over stubs, drippings, ashes and petals into the nearest body of water, lake or river.

Wrap the doll up and keep it securely away out of sight as a Love Binding Charm.

***

SPACE FOR YOUR NOTES/SPELLS/RITUALS FOR YOUR PERSONAL BOOK OF SHADOWS

THE WITCH'S ADVICE ON MONEY

Do not try to cast a Spell for Money unless you have a seed to plant. Nothing begets only nothing.

Casting a Spell for money when you have none will only produce an expanded state of same. Lack of money affirms poverty, no matter how hard you may try to deny that.

Spells call for a certain amount of money to be invested to procure the necessary ingredients. Money affirms money.

He who has, gets! He who has not, loses what he has! There is no getting around that Cosmic Law.

When one is barring the door against the ravenous Wolf of Poverty, it is very difficult to put oneself in the prosperous state of mind to be able to hook up with the Astrological Forces which rule the flow of cash and wealth.

It would be better to work under the influences of Mercury or Venus to attract opportunities and balance and harmony in life first, before one should work under Sol, or especially Jupiter, for money.

Solar and Jupiterian Rituals must first show harmony, balance and good cheer. Poverty level life does not allow that kind of mental state.

Jupiter Rituals expand the present set of circumstances. That is why inexperienced Spellcasters wonder why Money Spells under Jupiter only seem to make things worse.

To begin to lift oneself up and out of the quagmire of lack of money, be willing to work for it. Use the Mercurial Influences to bring jobs, fast luck in small amounts of cash, opportunities that can be attracted by Spells cast on Waxing Moon Days of Mercury.

Use the Venus Influence to keep the emotions in proper perspective with a harmonious home life, in order to remove the pressure and panic brought on by lack of material wealth.

Once the foundation has been laid and the work of self-improvement begun, the higher Forces will be more amenable to one's metaphysical manipulations.

Therefore, work with the minor Planetary Influences first, before trying to approach the major ones.

Mercury - Fast Luck, quick cash, opportunity, psychism. Wednesday
Venus - Love, harmony, emotional beauty. Fri.
Mars - Passion, energy, defense, attack. Tues.
Saturn - Binding, restrictions, lessons, justice (Cosmic). Sat.
Luna - Waxing: construction, initiation, growth; Waning: completion, elimination. Mon.
Sol- Health, good fortune, honors, balance, justice (Human). Sun.
Jupiter - Increased wealth, prosperity, moral right. Thurs.

AN OLD SOUTH RITUAL FOR SUCCESS

1 Green Jumbo Candle
1 Pink Jumbo Candle
1 Bottle Success Oil
1 Bottle Glow of Attraction Oil
1 Pkt. (1 lb.) Dragons Blood Bath Salt Crystals
1 Container Jinx-Removing Powder

Begin on a Sunday as the Moon waxes.

Anoint each candle with the Attraction Oil and burn them both for an hour each day until they are gone.

Daily, bathe with a tblsp. of Salt in your tube of hot bath water, and meditate on achieving the success you want.

Dust powder lightly in your shoes each day before going about your normal routine.

Anoint your hands each day with the Success Oil to turn all you touch into Success.

***

HIGH JOHN ROOT SPELL FOR MONEY AND SUCCESS

7 Green Candles
1 Bottle High John the Conqueror Oil
1 Packet " " " " Powder

SPACE FOR YOUR NOTES/SPELLS/RITUALS FOR YOUR PERSONAL BOOK OF SHADOWS

1 Packet " " " " Root
1 Pot of boiling water

Begin this work on a Thursday as the Moon waxes.

Anoint one candle with the oil and light it to burn out.

Set the root to rest beside the candle.

Sprinkle a pinch of the powder into the candle flame and another pinch or two into the steaming water. Wave the hands back and forth through the steam as you concentrate on attracting financial gain and chant:

MONEY THERE, MONEY HERE, MONEY IN MY HAND.
STACKS OF CASH AND BILLS IN A BAND,
COME HERE TO ME FROM THROUGHOUT THE LAND.

Vision yourself drawing whatever amounts of money you need for a particular endeavor.

Repeat each day until all seven candles are gone.

Thereafter, carry the Root on the person as a Money and Success Drawing Charm.

***

A MONEY DRAWING HOODOO

7 Green Candles
7 Yellow Candles
7 Brown Candles
1 Bottle Money Oil
1 Packet Money Powder
1 Packet Money Incense
1 Parchment Square, 2 x 2

Begin on Wednesday as the Moon waxes.

Anoint one candle of each color with the oil and scribe the amount of money needed on the parchment.

Set the three anointed candles to form a triangle and light them. Place the packet of powder close by.

Set the parchment in the center of the three candles and light a bit of Incense to burn as you say:

MONEY COMETH FROM FAR AND NEAR,
MONEY PILETH UP RIGHT HERE.
WORDS BE SIMPLE, WORDS BE PLAIN,
DRAWETH FOR ME FINANCIAL GAIN.
WILL AND WORDS SWEET AS HONEY,
BRINGETH TO ME ALL KINDS OF MONEY!.

Allow the candles and the incense to burn out. Repeat the same process with three fresh candles until all are gone; that is, one of each color, each night thereafter.

Then the powder must be lightly dusted around the place which is the source of your income - job, employment interview, gambling casino, etc.

Wear, thereafter, the parchment square in your left shoe, as a Money Drawing Charm.

***

A SIX DAY RITUAL FOR MONEY

6 Gold Candles, 42 Green Candles,
54 White candles
1 Lg. Bottle of Money Oil, Crown of Success Oil or Power Oil
1 oz. of Frankincense Tears
1 Packet of Blessed Salt
6 Charcoals
1 $5.00 bill
1 $1.00 bill

On a Day of Sol, as the Moon waxes, fold up the Bills and set them crosswise in the center of your Altar.

Anoint a gold candle with the oil and place it on top of the money.

Ring the gold candle with 7 of the green, after they have been well anointed with the oil also. Surround that with a circle of 9 white candles, which also have been anointed.

As each candle is being anointed, see in your Mind's Eye, money being attracted to you.

Sprinkle a ring of salt around the entire formation.

Set a bit of the Frankincense to burn on a coal and invoke the Power of one of the Classical Sun Gods, such as Sol, Shamash,

SPACE FOR YOUR NOTES/SPELLS/RITUALS FOR YOUR PERSONAL BOOK OF SHADOWS

Apollo, Ra, Baldur, etc. to attend upon your Rite and lend aid.

See your blessings of Wealth as coming to you.

Light the first gold candle, then all 7 greens and finally all 9 of the whites. Move widdershins in lighting the green and white candles.

Speak out this incantation as the gold is lit and again as the first green is lit and a third time as the first white is lit:

ALL THE SUN GODS OF FORTUNE AND WEALTH,
BRING ME BLESSING, JOY AND HEALTH!
FINANCES AND PROSPEROUS ESTATE
PILED NEATLY WITHIN MY GATE.
I SEE MONEY, I SEE GOLD,
I SEE DOLLAR, MARK AND POUND,
BANKNOTES FLY AROUND AND AROUND.
BLESS ME WITH GOOD LUCK IN MONEY,
MAKE MY LIFE FLOW WITH MILK AND HONEY!

Meditate on that idea for a good while and allow the candles to burn down and out.

Repeat the process for the next 5 days, until all the candles are gone. Thereafter, carry the folded Banknotes on your person as a Money Drawing Charm.

Scatter the left over wax and ashes to the Four Winds.

***

MONEY INCREASE SPELL

2 Green Candles
1 Packet High John Incense
1 Bottle High John or Money Oil
1 Piece of Parchment Paper
1 Lg. coin, 50¢, or Silver Dollar

On a Sunday, on or just after the New Moon, Wrap the coin in the parchment and set it before you.

Anoint the candles with the oil and set them to stand one on each side of the wrapped coin.

Burn a bit of the incense and light the candles.

See in your Mind's Eye money piling up in front of you. Vision that idea very clearly. Chant:

AS THE MOON DOTH GROW TO FULL,
LET THIS WORKING GENTLY PULL.
MONEY TO DRAW, MONEY TO GROW,
MONEY COMETH FAST, NOT SLOW!

After 1/2 hour, put the candles out and repeat the Spell one month hence on a Sunday at the New Moon and again one month hence from that at the same Day and Lunar Phase.

***

THE ANCIENT RITUAL FOR TURNING THE SILVER

14 White Taper Candles
1 Bottle Horn of Plenty Oil
1 Packet Wealthy Way or Money Incense
1 Lg. coin, 50¢, or Silver Dollar

On a Night of the New Moon, anoint one candle with the Oil.

Light the Candle and take it and the coin out of doors under the sky, to where you can gaze up to the heavens.

Bow 9 times to the Moon (in the direction of where the Moon ought to be, as She is dark on the Night of the New Moon.)

Repeat with each bow:

O GREAT MOVER OF THE TIDE,
BRING MONEY TO MY SIDE.

Hold out the strongest hand with the coin and have the lit candle in the other. Say:

I KEEP THIS ANCIENT TRYST WITH MONEY IN MY FIST.

Turn the coin over in your hand 9 times and say with each turning:

BLESS ME WITH PROSPERITY, O SILVERY GODDESS OF THE SEA!

SPACE FOR YOUR NOTES/SPELLS/RITUALS FOR YOUR PERSONAL BOOK OF SHADOWS

Take the coin and candle back indoors. Set the candle to burn on your Altar with the coin resting beside it.

Light a bit of the Incense and allow all to burn out.

Repeat this each night of the Waxing Moon, until She stands Full, using a fresh candle each Night.

Do this monthly until your financial state improves.

***

AN IMAGE DOLL CANDLE TO ATTRACT MONEY

1 Image Doll Candle to represent self, red, white or green
1 Bottle Personal Zodiac Oil; Libra, Taurus, etc.
1 Piece of Parchment
1 Packet ground Sunflower Petals and Marigold Flowers
1 Packet Sandalwood or Power Incense

On a Night of Sol, near the New Mon, anoint the candle with the Zodiac Oil to represent yourself in your Mind's Eye.

Sprinkle a goodly amount of the ground herbs on and around the Image.

Scribe the exact amount of money you need on the Parchment and stand the Image upon it.

Light the Candle and some of the Incense.

Vision the money coming to you as you chant over and over:

ALL PLANETARY POWERS TAKE HEED!
I HAVE FOR THIS AMOUNT A GREAT NEED.
THIS MONEY I MUCH DESIRE,
SEE MY WILL IN THE CANDLE FIRE.
THIS AMOUNT RIGHTFULLY MINE
COMES TO ME AT THE RIGHT TIME.

Vision yourself receiving the blessing of the amount of money you need for your immediate concerns.

After twenty minutes of this intense concentration, put the flame out. Repeat the procedure each night thereafter, until the candle is consumed.

Tear up the Parchment and scatter it outside with the Incense ashes to the Four Winds.

***

A GAMBLERS RITUAL

1 Green Candle
1 Piece of Parchment
1 Bottle of Sandalwood Oil

Sundays or Thursdays as the Moon waxes, anoint the candle with the oil and vision deeply your intention of winning money at Gaming.

Scribe the method of Gaming on the Parchment with a positive statement to the effect of being a Winner.

Light the Candle and burn the Parchment in the flame.

Vision yourself as being lucky while the candle burns for about an hour, before putting it out.

Take the stub in the left pocket and go to a Gaming House.

Finger the stub with the left hand in the pocket and dab a bit of the oil from the candle onto the things used in games of chance; money, slots, dice, chips, cards or tickets.

Your positive visioning goes before you and should aid your results.
(Author's Note: IF AT FIRST YOU DON'T SUCCEED, TRY, TRY AGAIN! One has to build up a positive attitude, in a habitual frame of mind. Do not play on scared money! One must be out for fun and not under pressure to win. Take it from one Witch who has lived in Las Vegas for 35 years.)

***

SPACE FOR YOUR NOTES/SPELLS/RITUALS FOR YOUR PERSONAL BOOK OF SHADOWS

THE WITCH'S PSYCHISM

The Ancient Art of Scrying--Mastery of the Crystal Ball

Scrying is an ability which may take considerable time to develop. Patient and perseverance, however, are the Watchwords.

In shopping for a Crystal Ball, only you can decide which size and cost is right for you. A particular one will call out to you. That one is yours.

Once having obtained your ball, you can set up your own regimen for training.

As you sit at the Crystal, you must be physically comfortable. Your entire system must be well balanced and at rest. The surface of the Crystal should be so placed it can be gazed upon without eye strain.

Pass your strongest hand over the Crystal as you hold it and charge it by Will to yourself and to your works of the Mercurial Arts. Never allow another person to touch it. When not in use, keep it covered with a special cloth of black velvet.

Your training sessions should be about the same time each day and last no longer than about 1/2 hour. The ability to "see" develops over a period of time.

Some Scryers say the clearest pictures come during the Waxing Moon. Experiment yourself, because some persons are affected adversely at that time and are at their best during the Wane.

At first the Crystal may seem to fade in and out of focus. This is caused by the relaxing and tightening of the eye muscles. Also a binding feeling in the head and a sensation known as "the Tickling of the Ant" may be felt.

These are caused by the circulation of the blood and the stimulation of the Pituitary Gland as it is activated. *These are good signs* and will pass with time.

It takes a while for psychic impressions to cut a new channel betwixt the Sub-conscious and Conscious levels in the Mind.

The Crystal will begin to show misty cloud formations which swirl and move. That stage will eventually pass and more clarity will show.

Then pictures and faces of persons and things will be seen, also landscapes and colors will show themselves, but only fleetingly, at best, in early stages.

Symbols will form. Do not try to interpret them, but continue to work at it and they will eventually take on a meaning for you.

As the Ancient Wizards say: *"Thy first type of vision cometh to thee through THE GATES OF IVORY. Though knowest then thou be on the right track and developeth as thou shouldst."*

This type is seen without any emotional atmosphere and you have no knowledge as to what it means.

The second type, *"Cometh to thee through THE GATES OF HORN and bringeth definite knowledge of its meaning."* It has an emotional flavor.

The knowledge which comes immediately following this type of vision can be relied upon to be true and correct.

If you develop fully enough to be able to help others with your scrying, you will then be able to pick up telepathic or "spirit" signals associated with your subject when you read for others.

Pose questions which have a bearing on the Querent's problem and concentrate. After a slight pause to scry, interpret the visions you receive.

In the beginnings of your career as a Seer, scry for others only on Nights of Mercury, as Luna waxes.

Use two white candles to set before you with the Crystal set between and slightly in front of them.

A bit of flickering light should fall on the Crystal as you scry. The dancing light helps your visionary channels to open.

Begin your sessions by lighting the two candles. Uncover the Crystal and pass your strongest hand over it. Light a Mercurial Incense, such as Benzoin and Mace.

Have a chalice of clear Water sitting at your left hand when sitting to scry. It blocks all adverse negative Psychic Influences.

Go into yourself and invoke thus:

SPACE FOR YOUR NOTES/SPELLS/RITUALS FOR YOUR PERSONAL BOOK OF SHADOWS

ODIN! ODIN! ODIN!
LORD OF MAGIC AND FABLE TRAGIC!
CASTER OF THE RUNES.
TELL US TRUE,
WHAT WE MUST DO.
WE SEEKETH THY WORDS AND BOONS.

Begin thereupon to scry until the mist begins to clear.

Ask your Querent, then, what he/she would know or have revealed.

It is a violation of Witch Law to refuse to give forth the truth of a vision, once it is given to you. You know not the whys and wherefores of the Gods. You are only a channel for the Psychic. Knowledge comes through you, not for you.

Fear not to speak out what you are shown. You know not how that fits into the situation of the Querent, but he/she does.

SCRY THY VISION WITH HONESTY AND PRECISION AND THY SEERSHIP WILT NEVER BRING DERISION.

***

Automatic Writing--Messages from the "Beyond"

This is an ancient method of receiving psychic messages, be they from "Spirit" or from deep levels of the Collective Unconscious.

On the Days or Nights of Mercury, as the Moon waxes, your early training in this field would be more easily facilitated.

Upon your brow anoint a Medium's or Spirit Channeling Oil and burn a soft Sandalwood, Jasmine or Wisteria Incense to set a pleasant mood.

You could have candles of yellow or light blue burning off to the side away from your direct view. Those are the main Mercurial colors.

Silently meditate on opening, on inner levels, a channel to the psychic, or Astral Plane.

Place your hand with pencil or pen on a paper upon the table before you. Rest comfortably and do not strain.

In your Will and with your Imagination cause your Astral or Etheric hand to pass through the table and rest upon your knee under the table.

That leaves the physical hand vacated and void so it may accept the influences from whatever Power or "Entity" who may wish to communicate.

Meditate on what you would know or ask of "Spirit." Allow to happen what does.

Nothing at first may happen.

With time and repeated effort, soon your writing hand will begin to move of its own accord and scrambled scrawls may come to the paper.

The messages will become clearer with experience and can be an accurate gauge of your psychic ability.

You would know you have succeeded in vacating the physical hand, by placing the etheric on your knee, because the physical will begin to feel cold.

When the session is over, do not neglect to will your etheric back into the physical.

Clap the hands thrice to scatter the vibes and restore mundane consciousness.

***

A FEW WORDS TO THE WISE ON PSYCHISM

In the Psychic Arts, so often one must open up to the influences from the outside, such as in Mediumship.

True Spiritual knowledge and Wisdom comes from the inside. Do not ever be a passive Psychic, by allowing oneself to be told what to do and how to act by any force or entity outside yourself.

They can be allowed to communicate, but not direct your actions. Be receptive to the "vibes," but also in control of yourself. Should ever a communicating Spirit make one feel uncomfortable, close the channel at once.

Beware of those that *ask* your permission before they can act or do anything for you. Their motives are evil.

Higher Entities do not need to ak, but will never do anything contrary to your Freedom of Choice. The Lower ones do not have any spiritual authority and need your consent to act on your behalf. Send them

SPACE FOR YOUR NOTES/SPELLS/RITUALS FOR YOUR PERSONAL BOOK OF SHADOWS

straight away, no matter how pleasant or flattering they are to you.

If you do not control them, they will control you.

FOREWARNED IS FOREARMED!

***

Ouija Boards--Intelligent Control Most Important

Do not be influenced by person who cry "Doom and Devils!" because of the Ouija. Those who say they feel Evil Beings possess the board however, may not be too far off the track, because it is a very easy method for lower entities to use. They must be intelligently controlled.

Perhaps the Doom-Sayers have seen those Unfortunate Souls who allow the board to control them!

As with anything else, those who go to extremes and abuse a thing may have resulting trouble. Do we say carrots are of the Devil because a few "Health Food Nuts" overdo it and OD on carrot juice?

I will illustrate with a good case in point, as to how a Ouija *is not* to be used:

Perhaps you know, or have seen a person such as this, under the Spell of the Ouija.

He/She works the Ouija alone. Unbalanced effort to begin with. Such a one passes the show pointer back and forth over the board and goes into trance.

The pointer begin, thereupon to move rapidly and flies over the board back and forth, not stopping on any letters.

The entranced Medium would say:
COME IN, MR. Y! COME IN, MR. Y!
YES, MR. Y IS HERE. MR. Y IS HERE...
ASK MR. Y ANYTHING YOU WANT TO KNOW...

Whereupon the "Control" supposedly gives Spiritual Advice to the Medium's Clients.

The deeper into trance the Medium goes, the faster the pointer moves on the board, not stopping anywhere. All the while, Mr. Y babbles his nonsense!

Plagues and Demons! Avoid such a "Reading!"

Many people would see the unhealthy attachment to a Mr. Y and would try to wean a poor Soul away and set him/her back in the realm of sanity. However, the habit of a Mr. Y can be much too great for the Medium to do without.

He/She would feel as nothing without a Mr. Y and would think no one would come to him/her as a Reader, if there were no longer a Mr. Y to depend on.

By forcing such a person to see what a Mr. Y is in reality, unmasked, can prove to no avail. It would make the Medium fall down and cry like a child whose candy were snatched away. It is the Lover and Possessor of the Medium's Soul. Without the "Control," the Medium feels he/she is and has nothing.

But!!!! How did a Mr. Y take control? The Medium allowed it to. He/She gave permission to allow It to act!

Therein lies the danger of the Ouija.

You as an entity living in the world are a Four-Planed Being. You have a Spiritual, a Mental, an Emotional, and a Physical point of grounding. Discarnate Entities do not! They do not have the good sense of a physical grounding and do not like you to know that you have authority over them. They must fall back and defer to your Will, when you impose it.

Let us now proceed to work the Ouija properly, *remaining in control*.

Before a session with a Ouija Board, scent your work area with a light Incense, perhaps Sandalwood or Honeysuckle. Keep a white, blue or yellow candle burning near your table.

Have a Chalice of Water to the left hand during any Psychic Session.

Work the Ouija only with another person as a partner to provide a complete and closed circuit, not leaving any open ends in your working.

It may be best to have a third person present to act as Scribe and write down the letters over which the pointer stops in passing. All three participants sign and date the scribed results, in case any portion prove prophetic.

SPACE FOR YOUR NOTES/SPELLS/RITUALS FOR YOUR PERSONAL BOOK OF SHADOWS

With the partner, place both hand's fingertips lightly on the pointer on the board. Go into a *light*, not deep, trance and speak a blessing on your work, dedicating it to the higher Forces of Spiritual Enlightenment. Meditate.

The pointer may then begin to move. Ask who the entity is who is making itself known.

Cold, discomfort, or answers crass and vile show an unenlightened Spirit. *Do not try to elevate such being to higher things.* There lies the danger of falling under its control. Thinking one is so spiritually adept as to be able to inspire negatives to strive for enlightenment, opens one up to vanity, which a negative will flatter, and one is lost.

If such negative things try to communicate, take your hands off the board to close the channel and *order it away*.

Feelings of love, joy and enlightened answers to your questions should be pursued. Question the entity, and record answers.

Do not, however, use the Ouija as a Parlor Game. It is a type of Oracle and deserves a modicum of proper respect.

Be prepared for any type of an answer, but maintain and openminded skepticism. Do not be overly impressed with the revealing entity. It does not have the Wisdom of the Ages, but only the limited knowledge of a discarnate Human Soul. It may be knowledgeable in certain fields, but is not privy to the designs of God/Goddesses, Creator/Creatrix Him/Herself.

When the entity leaves, or when you grow tired, remove the hands to break contact, closing the channel and clap thrice to change the atmosphere, even after a positive entity has communicated. You must restore normal consciousness in either case.

With such an attitude, *you* maintain control and may question the Spirit as it manifests. Prove all those who would speak to you from out of the Ouija. Make certain they are of the higher "Realms." Those of higher States of Being never try to abrogate your free Will and never suggest anything unworthy of Angelics.

When working an Oracle, such as the Ouija, keep your two feet firmly on the ground and the Mr. Ys will avoid you like the Black Death itself.

Blessed Be!

***

Psychometry -- The Art of Reading Vibrations

To read vibrations from things and persons was a psychic talent much employed in the Ancient World. Priestesses, and to some degree Priests, in the Shrines of the Old Gods used these Mystic Arts to help their communities.

The young person, male, but more particularly female, was dedicated at an early age when he/she showed signs of Seership. Heightened sensitivity was usually the key.

During the time the politically oriented Christian Clergy usurped spiritual leadership in the Western World, Divination was made to be anathema, and the strict codes of the example of the Hebrew Temple in old Jerusalem, as to patriarchal authority, was used to decry "Psychic" gifts throughout Christendom.

Most, if not all, organized hierarchical religious structures hate the fluid Psychism of Priestesses.

Divination and Psychism show the Spirit World and Inner Planes of Being not to be *what* and *as* the Clergy says. A Clergy's ploys for power and control of people's Minds will not impress those who know spiritual things.

Hence, the Old Religion had to be prevented from having an appeal in the hearts of the multitude.

Hence, the Devil was invented and made to be "Father of Lies" with *women in Psychism* as his minions.

Hence, the most dastardly deeds of the Christian Religion; the Witchcraft Mania.

Let us leave such a sad thought and allow Christianity to rue its own acts of hateful violence. The Old Religion resurgeth!

We no longer have the Outer Porticos of the Temples to train and develop the Seers and Seeresses. However, much may still be done by one developing alone.

Were you born into this world with a gentle nature which sees worth and value in

SPACE FOR YOUR NOTES/SPELLS/RITUALS FOR YOUR PERSONAL BOOK OF SHADOWS

Begin to develop your inner awareness by meditating on your concept of the God/Goddess, Creator/Creatrix.

Anoint your throat, brow and Solar Plexus with Deja Vu, Spirit Channeling or Sandalwood Oil and burn Mugwort as an Incense when you meditate.

Go out into Nature and commune with Wind, Sea, Mountain, Desert, Farm Land, Tree, Lake, River, etc.

Feel the vibrations and the messages they have to tell you. Sit by, or in them, allowing all care to drain away and out of you. Let them fill you with their voices and feelings.

Next, drain all tension and observe people as they go about their daily lives. Pick up what such feelings and "vibes" also tell you.

Impressions from those things and persons will begin to tell you very much. They may come to the head or to the Solar Plexus. Allow them to enter and speak to you.

Joy and Sadness, wonder and woe, experience them all.

Thirdly, take up objects from Nature and handle them. Go into yourself and try for an At-One-Ment with them. Their tales will unfold for you.

Fourthly, apply that ability to objects from persons, having been in close proximity to them for periods of time. They will unfold tales of stronger vibes.

Place the object against your forehead or Solar Plexus, quiet the mind and empty the feelings. Sense out to the object and try to connect with it.

Speak out exactly what picture comes to mind, or what feelings well up in you. Do not reason it out. If you do, the First Impressions will weaken and not be vivid and reliable.

The "Yes, but No!" Psychic is seldom valid.

Fifthly, when you presume to give "Readings" by Psychometry for others, you should burn a bit of Mugwort before hand to help open psychic channels, by breathing in the fumes.

Keep a goblet of Water at your left hand during a reading. Have a white, blue or yellow candle gently lighting the area. Thus do three of the Ancient Elements of the Wise help; Air, Fire and Water produce Earth, which is the Manifestation you would bring about, your portend or prognostication.

***

Scrying, Automatism and Psychometry are the three Powers of the Witches of Old.

Work them well, within the bonds of good taste. Know and Beware! Your Power as a Seer will be lauded and sought after by many.

Some are impressionable and suggestible. They would want your leave to visit the WC and would also ask your leave to flush! That places great power in your hands over them.

Unethical manipulation of others for your own ego and/or unreasonable financial gain brings you into the Realm of the Black Magician.

The Lords of Karma will never be cheated!

Do not allow any to fix an unhealthy dependency on you, as a Reader, to the exclusion of common sense.

What you may see in "Spirit" for your Querents is only the most logical conclusion of their present course of action, good or ill. At any moment in Time and Space, each one may choose a different path to take, leading to a different "Future." Divination only helps one assess the Past and the Present, to be able to arrange the Future and navigate more advantageously. Let each Querent be the Captain of His/Her own Soul.

In that way, you become a Seer or Seeress in the best traditions of the Ancient Wisdom Religion of the Old Gods.

SPACE FOR YOUR NOTES/SPELLS/RITUALS FOR YOUR PERSONAL BOOK OF SHADOWS

THE ETHICS OF HEXEREI

The Craft has had an age old Tradition which has come to be called, or associated with, "the Somber Man in black." It has always been a nebulous figure who shows up, almost out of nowhere, summoning the Witches to gather and to re-affirm their Arts and Ancient Faith.

He then disappears and is not seen, nor heard from, again for perhaps generations.

He usually is accompanied by a large black dog, or sometimes a strange bird. Never cats. Cats belong to the female aspect of the Craft and are usually associated with Witch women.

The Man in Black has been known to take a few serious students under his wing, teaching them the Ancient Arts. He has not the time for those who "dabble" and who are not totally committed to the Occult.

He will arrive in a town, create quite a stir among the local Practitioners of Magic and Witchcraft. He will mix and make authentic Charms and Spell ingredients, do a few good "Readings," leaving his Querents breathless and amazed, and vanish with the Night Wind just as mysteriously as he came.

He will leave, however, something very important behind him: Ethics In Magic!

Magical Ethics has always been a sticky problem for many in the Occult Field. To an Old Swain, such as the Man In Black, and those of his students, morals and ethics are what *you* make them.

Most things in Nature and in Spirit are neutral and bear no moral responsibility whatsoever. Magic is one of those things.

One can fill a bath tub with water to relax and bathe, or one can use the full tube to drown one's old Aunt Minnie. Is the water to blame for its use?

Therein lies the key to what is "White or Black" Magic. Only the individual ethical bent of the Practitioner him/herself determines the positive or negative bent of the Art.

One must be willing to accept the responsibility and/or consequences of one's actions as one navigates within the framework of the Law of Compensation (Karma), established by the God/Goddess, Creator/Creatrix. There is no way of evading their Judgement and the working out of the immutable Laws of Life.

Magic used for blessing and love produce after their kind with the good things of this World. That used for darker motivations also brings such to the Practitioner.

If the benefit from a dark working is worth the compensation one must pay, and one is sure one is justified in revenge, the darker Magics may be employed. One will, however, have to pay the price for it.

No one is so good or "angelic" that angry dark thoughts have not tempted one to try a Hex, in a fleeting moment in the mind.

On one's death bed there is no way one can cry: "Jesus Saves!" and expect a lifetime of negative action to be erased. Only by the slow and steady working out of one's own payment and just deserts can the negatives be turned into positives.

Be that as it may, Dark Magics exist and are used and employed. One must make one's own choice in the matter. There is, however, one catch:

MAKETH THINE OWN CHOICE, TAKETH THINE OWN RESPONSIBILITY, BUT ABIDETH THEREWITH!

***

THE WITCH'S HAND OF POWER

Psychological effect is very important in works of the dark side. To deliver a Curse verbally to one's enemy can be half the battle won. The thought of woe and misery planted into the mind of an enemy, by forceful gesture and words of malediction, may often help bring the victim into a fearful depression, allowing the Spell, which follows up, to be more effective.

Face the enemy/victim with a calm manner and exterior. Internally, however, be a boiling inferno of rage.

Make and keep eye contact as the left arm is extended at the person and close the right eye to stare intently down the left arm with the left eye, as the index and middle

SPACE FOR YOUR NOTES/SPELLS/RITUALS FOR YOUR PERSONAL BOOK OF SHADOWS

fingers of the left hand are pointed at him/her, clenching the others tight as a ball.

Spew forth with a devastating string of maledictions pronouncing woe, misery and tormet to come, at the victim/enemy.

Then, calmly without further word, walk briskly away to set about preparing a Hex properly suited to the case at hand.

Do not allow the effect of the dramatic atmosphere, thus created, to simply dissipate unused.

This was a method of Malediction employed by the Druids of Old to great effect, because their contemporaries knew they would do whatever was necessary to keep their words. Do not use it lightly.

Evoked energy must be properly expended, or you become impotent in all aspects of Magic.

***

TO WORK A BLACK CANDLE

Perhaps no aspect of the Occult causes as much "gut-feeling" fear as the idea of a Black Candle. It has been associated with evil Sorcery and Hexcraft for many years.

Actually, without an evil, adverse, or negative intention, or without any charge being laid on the candle at all, a Black Candle will simply astringe the atmosphere and clear away negative feelings and/or forces.

A Black Candle takes on its evil or sinister reputation only after it has been impregnated with a negative wish for ill-Will by being "dressed" with an Occult Oil of negative association, and stroked over and over again having the "curse" infused into it by the magnetism of an ill-wisher visualizing the effect to be placed on the victim against whom the candle is to be burned.

As with all candle-burning procedures: IF THE SUBJECT/VICTIM KNOWS THAT MAGIC IS BEING PERFORMED AND SHARES THE SAME BELIEF SYSTEM AS THE PRACTITIONER/SORCERER, BEYOND A DOUBT, IT WILL SURELY WORK.

The color of a candle, in itself, is neutral until the mind of a Practitioner of Candleburning activates it and charges the burning candle to be a focusing lens for the intention of an Occult Working.

It is the correspondence black has with the "Saturine" Force to restrict, bind, thrwart and impede that has made the Black Candle so fearsome in the Occult Arts.

However, it takes an Adept to be able to properly employ one effectively. Hexerei is not an aspect of the Art for the Neophyte or "Dabbler." **Only the stout of heart should dare.**

The method Adepts use to employ a Black Candle takes a bit of a flair in the Art Magical.

At the proper Astrological Time; id est, a Night of Saturn, under a Waning Moon, and if at all possible, as She passes in an Earth Sign, take the candle into your weakest hand, that is the secondary one, and the Occult Oil to anoint or "dress" the candle into the strongest, or most dominant one.

With the Oil, being a Fluid Condenser of Thought, proceed to stroke the Oil onto the candle from the bottom to the top, visioning the type of results you would have brought about, for a full five minutes holding steady that one thought.

Any chant made up to embody that idea may accompany this act.

The candle itself will begin to feel heavier to the hand slightly after this act of mental charging is given to it.

Then it is considered "dressed" and ready for use in an Occult Spell or Ritual.

The stroking from the bottom to the top is symbolic of sending a Hex or Bane from the Spellcaster to the Subject/Victim. It is also the direction of dressing candles used to lift Curses or Jinxes and send things away.

Love or Money Candles should be dressed with Oil and Intent from the top to the bottom, symbolic of attracting a blessing or boon.

***

THE PRINCIPLE OF THE BLACK FAST

The ancient Irish Curse: "I'll fa[illegible] thy Doorstep!" was an effective me[illegible] bringing pressure to bear on an ene[illegible] had done one definite wrong.

SPACE FOR YOUR NOTES/SPELLS/RITUALS FOR YOUR PERSONAL BOOK OF SHADOWS

It was done publically for the entire Community to know that the Faster had been wrongfully injured by the person against whom the Fast was being held.

When you are wrongly put upon by one who bears you ill-Will, procure 9 Black Jumbo Candles, 1 bottle Black Arts Oil, 1 packet Black Arts Incense and 1 piece of parchment paper.

Traditionally, it was started on a Friday, under a Waning Moon, to bring the pressure of the Black Fast upon a Nemesis.

Anoint one candle with the Oil and light it after charging it to be your hatred toward the one who did you wrong.

Light some of the Incense with the intention of affecting that one adversely as you would wish.

Scribe your curse smartly on the parchment and set it beneath the candle.

Fast the entire day and night, brooding your curse against that one as the candle burns. Allow it to consume itself.

Repeat the Fast each Friday for a total of 9 Weeks. As the last flame of the last candle flickers out, burn the parchment in it.

Your intense feeling should cause movement in the Ether to bring your just reward.

Let it be known the Black Fast in is progress.

***

TO BIND THY BUSINESS COMPETITION

1 Jumbo Brown Candle
1 Bottle Master Oil
1 Parchment Square, 2x2

Early on a Night of Saturn, as Luna be on the wane, anointeth the candle with the oil and vision thy rival as not having any business.

Goeth to his/her Shop or place of business and smeareth a bit of the oil on the door frame.

Scribe his/her name on the parchment and placeth it in an ice tray with fresh water.

Setteth that in thy freezer and sayeth:

ICE AND COLD ON THEE TAKE HOLD!
FREEZE IN ICE AS LONG AS I PLEASE!
NO MORE TO ADVANCE, NO MONEY TO ENHANCE!
BE GRIPPED IN A VICE, 'TILL I BEAT THEE BY THRICE!

Keepeth his/her name in the ice until thou hast gotten ahead of the situation. Leave the candle to burn out and casteth the stub away.

***

AN OLD WITCH'S DEVILISH FIRE

1 Jumbo Black Candle
1 Bottle Black Arts or XX Oil
1 Packet Black Arts or Crossing Incense
1 item of the victim's clothing, recently worn

Await a Night of Saturn, as the Moon be on the wane and anointeth the candle with the oil, brooding thy heavy curse upon thy victim.

Lighteth a bit of the incense and sayeth:

DARK FIENDS OF DEEPEST NIGHT, GATHER HERE ON WINGED FLIGHT!

Wrappeth the candle in the piece of garment and setteth it to stand in a tub, fireplace or out of doors.

Lighteth the candle to burn and vision silently the woe and misery for thy victim until the clothing catcheth ablaze. Then shouteth:

UP, FIENDS, TO BLAZE AND BURN!
MAKE _________ WRITHE AND CHURN!
TORMENT MOST DIRE,
BY BLACK CANDLE FIRE!
MAIM AND SCORCH AND DEVASTATE,
MAKE _________ TRULY REPROBATE!
RETURNETH NOT TO THY ABODES MOST DEEP,
'TIL I HEARETH _________'S DYING PEEP!

Alloweth the candle and clothing to be consumed by fire as thou dost vision thy curse falling upon the victim.

SPACE FOR YOUR NOTES/SPELLS/RITUALS FOR YOUR PERSONAL BOOK OF SHADOWS

Leaveth the ashes and melted was where he/she wilt surely see it.

***

CANDLES IN THE GRAVE

3 Black Jumbo Candles
1 Bottle Witches Formula Oil of Confusion
1 Packet Black Arts or Cobra Incense

Proceedeth to a Cemetery with thy ingredients on a Night of Saturn near to the Dark of the Moon.

Findeth a fresh grave newly covered over.

Lighteth thy Incense in a bowl of earth and sayeth:

POWERS OF THIS DREADFUL PLACE
SHOW UNTO ME THY MOURNFUL FACE!
ACCEPTETH THIS ONE I GIVETH TO THEE
THINE TO TORMENT, THINE TO BE!

Placeth the candles to stand side by side and lighteth each with these words:

ONE FOR THE BODY, ONE FOR THY SOUL
AND ONE FOR THY MIND,
THAT THOU GIVETH FORTH THY SPIRIT
AND LEAVETH THIS WORLD BEHIND!

Slowly dost thou begin to push dirt from the grave over the candles until they be buried.

Taketh the oil to thy victim's door and smeareth the frame therewith.

Thy intense ill-will shouldst surely take affect.

***

TO BLIGHT AN AFFAIR

3 Black Candles
3 Red Candles
1 Bottle Saturn Oil
1 Bottle Mars or Dragons Blood Oil
1 Packet Patchouli Incense
1 Packet Nettle, Rue, Black Mustard and Dill, to a 1/2 oz. each.

Placeth thy Chalice in the center of thy Altar on a Night of Saturn, as the moon waneth.

Anointeth the black candles with the Saturn Oil and standeth them around the Chalice.

Anointeth the red candles with the Mars Oil and placeth them around between the black ones.

Lighteth thy Incense to burn and placeth a few pinches of the mixed herbs in the Chalice.

Lighteth only the black candles to burn as thou chanteth over and over:

ENMITY AND DISCORD RIFE,
__________ AND __________ SHANT BE MAN AND WIFE!
DEEP AFFLICTION
HERE UPON THIS BONDED PAIR!
DEMONS AND FRIGHTS
COME TO THESE LIGHTS,
SPEED UPON THE THICK NIGHT AIR!
DISCORD AND STRIFE,
STIFLE ALL LIFE,
MAKE THEIR LOVE WROUGHT WITH CARE!

Brood thy ill-will 'till the candles be gone.

On the following Night of Mars, as the Moon also waneth, boileth water and poureth it into the Chalice to brew the herbs, as thou lighteth the red candles to burn only 15 minutes saying:

MAY NO JOY EVER BE UNITED.
MAY THEY ALWAYS BE CROSSED AND BLIGHTED.
ERE A YEAR HATH GONE AWAY,
LET THEIR LIFE BE AS I SAY!

Alloweth the herbs to steep. Strain and bottle up the brew.

Thou must somehow contrive to induce a few drops into food the two will share.

At that time, maketh sure the red candles burn themselves out.

***

SPACE FOR YOUR NOTES/SPELLS/RITUALS FOR YOUR PERSONAL BOOK OF SHADOWS

JINX-REMOVING SPELLS

Curses and Hexes are not recommended for the Student of Occultism to use and bandy about unwisely.

Many persons shrink from that aspect of the Occult altogether and try not to even hear about such methods.

However, that puts them at a disadvantage when and if a notorious Magician of unethical means sets out to make life difficult for them.

Do not be deceived! When you begin to be a Force in Occult Studies, even for what you consider to be "good" or positive, you do and will come to the notice of certain persons of not so altruistic bent.

Cursings and Hexerei are very much a part of the Occult World, no matter how much one may protest to the contrary.

Some persons, albeit deluded and misguided, do cast Hexcraft for many reasons. Therefore, it is necessary to know Hexcraft in order to protect and deflect and reverse such negative works.

Occult Pollyanas, who sing hearts and flowers and swear they never engage in negative things, can and *do* leave themselves wide open to attacks by the unscrupulous and the Black Magician.

When it becomes known that you are knowledgeable in the Occult, certain types of individuals will try to play The Wizard's Ball Game with you, just to see if you are worth your stuff.

It is usually Ego and lust for Power that distinguishes such persons. They want to impose their mark on your Psyche, to let you know you are nothing in their eyes. They seem to have a need to be known, and felt to be an imposing presence in Occult Circles.

That kind of attitude leads to their eventual downfall.

How can you work against evil Hexerei, if you do not know how it is accomplished in the first place?

Contempt for others, ego-inflated desire for power, and under-estimation of another Practitioner, usually accomplish their own ruin.

A Black Magician would have such a low esteem for you, that he/she would normally not take precautions to prevent your positive magics being able to lift and send back Hexes. Black Magic is easily defeated.

Evil sorcery can not withstand a positive confrontation for any extended period of time. Negativity is intense and works very quickly, but soon evaporates from its inability to sustain the effort.

Eventually it is overcome and absorbed into the positive background of the Cosmic Universe as a whole and becomes the compost for bigger and better things to follow. So much for evil Wizards!

A Black Magician operates on fear. The fear he/she creates for him/her self in others, and his/her own *paranoia*.

It takes enormous effort to cause others to fear and more effort to constantly be on the defensive against the possibility of magical retaliation. A Black Magician can sustain a magical attack only on a limited scale.

He/She fights on two fronts at once and can and will be worn down by persistent and bold, sustained effort. After all, the positive Practitioner has all the energy of the Cosmos on which to call, and no time limit in which to use it.

One thing, however, you must not do, is pity the Black Magician. You must proceed against him/her relentlessly, applying positive force against negative. Negativity will always be forced to give place. That is Cosmic Law. Maintaining a healthy frame of mind, healthy vital energy, and positive attitude and common sense self-worth, will do more to prevent an attack of Black Magic than anything else.

An evil Sorcerer will try to gain access to your inner mind by pressing on your Psychic Centers with a strong Thought-Form. If you are not in a healthy vitality, you may feel the heat or tingling sensations of something trying to invade your being.

Hold the thumbs of each hand in the center of the palms of the opposite hands. If you can, sit down and cross the feet. This position closes you off, as a contained circuit, and prevents any energy loss the Black Magician is trying to drain away.

SPACE FOR YOUR NOTES/SPELLS/RITUALS FOR YOUR PERSONAL BOOK OF SHADOWS

Then silently, begin to breathe steadily and deeply to restore and charge up the aura.

When you feel at peak, project that energy out and at the direction from whence the creeping evil seems to be coming. The Evil One will receive a blast not expected.

Then close off again with the thumbs and crossed feet and remain silent until the feel of the danger has drained away. The Black Magician will have to slink back to the darkness and mull over what happened.

The thumb-holding technique is age old and has been used by many Practitioners to prevent adverse energy sent by one of evil intent from gaining access into one's being.

Ritual Ablutions are another means to ward off and keep negative energies at bay. They are Ritual bathing and Spiritual Acts of Cleansing. They are a series of Ritual Immersions in Bath Water to which Blessed Salt and Herbs, either in bulk or by Essential Oil, have been added.

The metaphysical idea being that of certain scents can give a positive power to one's own vital energy, in the aura, which prevent hostile intent from the malice of evil wizards affecting one adversely.

Bath crystals scented with Wisteria, Sandalwood, Almond, Heliotrope, Jasmine or Vetivert would be ideal to use in Ritual Ablutions.

Those Herbal Scents have a correspondence to establish positive energies and lift negative psychic intent.

A Ritual Bath would entail those Bath Crystals poured into the hot bath water and total immersions, perhaps three times, for a period of about eight minutes. Meditations or prayers are said to ward off and/or lift jinxed, crossed or hexed conditions in one's life. Then one must air dry, rather than towel dry with an herbal scented bath.

One's body and aura would then have the uplifting quality of the herbal essences and act as a barrier to keep ill-wishing away.

The astrological forces used to remove jinxes would be Mercury, under a waxing Moon, in an Air Sign.

On those days or nights the occult energies are much more conducive to the processes of lifting negative thoughts and/or crossed conditions put upon one by the dark intentions of an evil Wizard or Sorcerer/ess.

The nasty or evil intentions can be readily lifted and sent back to fester in the mind which conceived them. When Black Magic is properly deflected, it returns along the line of least resistance to its point of origin.

What the Black Magician had in mind for the victim manifests in his/her own circumstances. That is the just reward any abuser of the Occult Arts should receive.

***

A RITUAL TO REVERSE CURSES AND HEXES

3 Yellow or White Candles
1 Bottle Witchbane, Jinx-Removing or Uncrossing Oil
1 Packet Hermes Incense

On a Day of Mercury, as Luna waxes in an Air Sign, light a bit of the Incense and say:

SPIRITS OF THE ELEMENTS OF AIR
GATHER TO THIS CENSE MOST FAIR.
DRIVE OUT ALL DEMONS OF DARKER MIEN,
DISPELL THE HATE OF GALL AND SPLEEN

Anoint the three candles with the oil and vision the intentions of all evil thought returning to the one who sent them.

Anoint also the victim upon whom the negative attack was directed on the forehead, throat and chest, to lift the evil effects.

Light one of the candles and pass it thrice around the victim's head. Then circumambulate him/her thrice with the burning incense, moving deosil, as these words are spoken:

NIGHT BE DAY!
SEND EVIL AWAY!
COLD BE WARM!
NO EVIL SWARM!
DARK BE LIGHT!
ALL HEXEREI TAKE FLIGHT!
POWER OF THE AIR SPRITES,

SPACE FOR YOUR NOTES/SPELLS/RITUALS FOR YOUR PERSONAL BOOK OF SHADOWS

REVERSE ALL ADVERSE FRIGHTS.
SEND BACK TO THE EVIL ONE,
TO HIDE FROM LIGHT OF SUN.
IT SHALL BE AS IF NO MORE,
ALL EVIL FLEE FROM THIS VERY DOOR!

Allow the candle and incense to burn themselves out.

Repeat this each day thereafter for two more days, until the three candles are gone. The delivered victim should wear the oil as a body cologne until signs of the reversal are apparent.

***

TO REVERSE A SPELL

3 White Candles
1 Bottle Mercury Oil
1 Packet Compelling Incense

On a Day of Mercury, as Luna waxes in an Air Sign, anoint the three candles with the oil and set them in a row to stand North to South.

Set the Incense to burn and concentrate on reversing any thought that has been conjured and sent out.

Light the candles from North to South and chant:

BE STOPPED! BE TURNED! BE RIGHTLY BURNED!
REVERSE THE FLOW OF SPELLS SINCE CAST!
REVERSE THE AFFECT RIGHT SMART AND FAST!
LET ALL BE TURNED TO NAUGHT AND NILL!
ONLY THE OPPOSITE MY THOUGHTS SHALL FILL!

Vision the affect of Magical Works being reversed until the candles are reduced to mere stubs.

Snuff them out in reverse order of lighting; South to North.

Scatter the stubs and ashes to the Four Winds.

***

SPACE FOR YOUR NOTES/SPELLS/RITUALS FOR YOUR PERSONAL BOOK OF SHADOWS

THE CHAMBER OF HECATE

How To Work
A Coven Of
Three

AN INVOCATION TO HECATE

Hail, Dark Mother of the Waning Moon,
come to me as I chant this rune.
Cold Winds and dark hard Stone,
Waning Light and bleached Bone.
Summon She who walketh by Night,
whose shrieking voice causeth fright.
Hecate of evil mien
Bringeth Spirits from the deep Unseen.
Attend to this dark working dire,
Illumined by black Candle Fire.
With Mullein and Mugwort and herbs of rue,
Aid my will in this witchy brew.
Hecate come and bring Thy bane
Like falling hale and driving rain.
Hecate, of visage most dour,
Work my Will in this evil Hour!

SPACE FOR YOUR NOTES/SPELLS/RITUALS FOR YOUR PERSONAL BOOK OF SHADOWS

CEREMONIAL PROCEDURE

The power of three minds in concert, working on an Occult Problem can be a formidable force with which to reckon.

Three is the mystic number of Creation, or Eternity. When a thing is done in sequences of three, it is done symbolically, an infinite number of times.

A Coven of three, becomes, therefore, a potent element to work Magic, with the power of three minds intently bent and in one accord to bring the Forces of Magic, forth from the Mind, to bear upon a problem at hand.

The Coven should have either two females and one male, or two males and one female to function most effectively. However, a group of three, all of the same gender can also be effective, if all three can blend together well in the working of Magic.

It should be a robed Coven, with formal black ceremonial attire, uniform, with hood. Perhaps the symbol of the Waning Moon could be displayed on the chest.

The robe should be girded with a cingulum of purple to stand for mastery over the Spirit Realm.

An Altar Drape and Altar Candle should also be purple and the Ritual Chamber itself should be decorated in both black and purple to give forth the vibrations of Hecate, Ancient Goddess of Magic and Sorcery.

The Chamber should have a large symbol of the Waning Moon upon the North Wall, to be faced across the Altar by the three participants in the Rituals and Ceremonies.

In the center of the floor should be a 9 ft. Circle scribed in white and clearly defined as a permanent fixture.

In the center of the Circle should stand a square table about waist high to serve as the Altar. (See Diagram)

All three participants should be duly initiated Witches, of at least several years experience in the Craft, who know the methods of heavy ceremonial works.

Those who are inexperienced, and those who only "dabble" in the Occult are discouraged from attempting these works.

Sorcery is truly a game of Wizards and only adept Wizards and Wizardesses are encouraged to play it.

With that in mind, Magic can be properly worked in good order, leading to Mastery in the Great Art.

Each one of the three participants contribute to the working of a Ritual by handling some portion of the Spell or Ceremony being conducted; for instance, one could cast the Circle, opening the Ritual, one could perform the meat of the ceremony by casting the Spell using the necessary paraphernalia called for. All three would join together in raising the Power and sending it to work the group Will, and then the third member could close the Circle in proper order. That way each invests his/her energy to the working.

The particulars as to who does what, can be left to the group to work out itself.

Such has been the basic format and outline. It will be assumed, those who choose to follow this tome, have some knowledge of Magic, *so no concessions to amateurs* will be made.

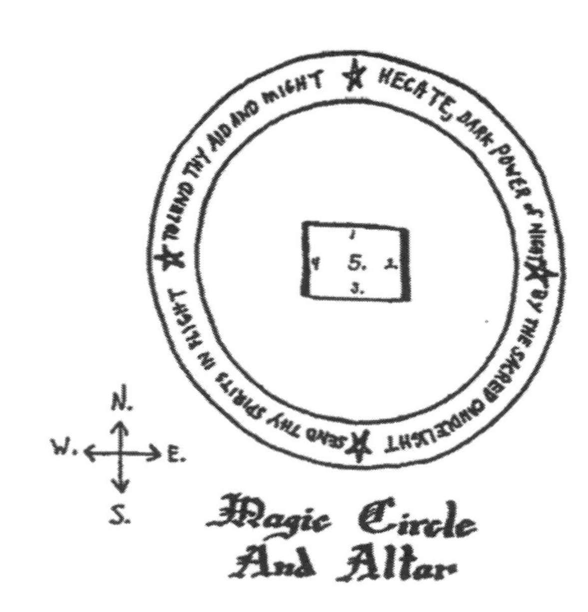

Magic Circle
And Altar

SPACE FOR YOUR NOTES/SPELLS/RITUALS FOR YOUR PERSONAL BOOK OF SHADOWS

Scribed on the floor of the Chamber, or in the bare Earth, should Ceremonies be done out of doors, the Circle should be at least 9 ft. in diameter of the inner Circle, giving the participants enough room in which to move.

On the Altar in space #1 rests a dish of Salt or Earth. In #2 is a Thurible to burn coals and Incense. #3 contains a purple Altar Candle, Jumbo size and the Athame, the ceremonial blade. #4 is for a Chalice of Water.

As can be seen, the Four Mystic Elements are present on the Altar for each working.

Space #5 is the center and would hold the necessary items used for any Spell to be worked.

At the four Quarters around the Circle are Pentagrams, as can be seen in the diagram. In those points would sit candles, either purple or black, to be the lights of the traditional Watch-Towers. Their holders may be of brass or earthenware.

The candle in space #3, on the Altar, would already be lit before a ceremony is to commence. From it coals for Incense would be lit and the candles in the Quarter points also.

It would be best for the group to maintain a proper Ritual Chamber, if possible, and hold the workings of the Coven indoors, away from the prying eyes of the crass and vulgar. However, some may wish to hold Ceremonies out of doors, in Nature, under wind and sky.

In that case, the Circle, its points and scribed words would be scratched in the Earth with a sharp stick. It must, however, be well smoothed over and erased after a Ritual Working is finished. No traces of the Craft should ever be left for the Stranger to find, indicating the whereabouts of Coven activity.

The opening procedure for the Circle will be given as The Casting. It is a three part system of circumambulations With Air (Incense), Fire (Altar Candle) and Blade (Athame).

The meat of the Spell or Ritual would then be done and the Closing would also follow a three point working to take down the Circle.

TO CAST THE MAGIC CIRCLE OF ART

At the proper time to conduct the Ritual, the Altar would be set with all necessary items to be used. The Altar Candle in space #3 would be burning and a lit coal for Incense would be in the Burner or Thurible.

The three Witches approach the Altar and stand facing North across it. All are serious and silent.

One, who is to do The Casting, takes some Incense and places it upon the live coal.

The Incense used to cast the Circle may be the same as to be used during the Spell, to follow, or may be a special Altar Incense of Benzoin, Mace and Frankincense.

The one to cast takes up the Burner and moves around and away from the Altar, passing widdershins to the North Quarter.

The Burner is held high and these words intoned:

POWERS OF THE NIGHT AND SKY, GATHER IN THE TWINKLING OF AN EYE!

The Incense is passed by moving widdershins in a total circumambulation from North to North again. A bow is made on passing the North the second time and the Burner returned to its place on the Altar.

He/She then takes up the Altar Candle and moves again to the North Quarter and lights the candle there, for the Watch-Tower. Holding the Altar Candle high, he/she says:

LIGHT THE WATCH-TOWERS OF THE QUARTERS FOUR. SUMMON MAGICS TO STAND AT THE DOOR.

He/She moves again widdershins around to the other Quarters of the Circle, lighting the other candles, repeating the intonation.

Then the Altar Candle is set back in place and the Blade taken up.

With the Blade, the Witch moves again to the North Quarter, inscribes an Invoking Pentagram in the Air at that Quarter and intones:

SPACE FOR YOUR NOTES/SPELLS/RITUALS FOR YOUR PERSONAL BOOK OF SHADOWS

COME, O LADY OF DARKEST MIEN,
HECATE, QUEEN OF NIGHT,
ATTEND THE WORKING OF MYSTIC RITE.

The Circle is again circumambulated widdershins and the same gesture and words repeated at each Quarter, with a final bow to the North as it is passed, returning to the Altar.

He/She rests the Blade back in its place and all three Witches intone in unison:

WE ARE HERE IN THE CHAMBER OF ART
TO HONE OUR WILL SHARP AS A DART.
WITCHES WORKS OF GREAT POWER AND INTENT,
SEND MAGICS AND SORCERY HEAVEN BENT.

The action of The Casting encloses the three inside a Circle of Will, suspended in the Astral, linking the Spiritual and Material Planes.

The three meditate quietly for a few moments to link up with the summoned image of Hecate.

When the Presence is felt to be strong in the area of the Circle, the Second Witch will state the nature of the Spell and the Purpose for the working to follow. (It may be a Love Spell, a Money Increase Spell, a Blessing for self or friends, a Healing, or a Hex or Curse)

Whichever it may be, the purpose, intent and reason must be justly stated for the summoned Power and Force to hear.

The Second Witch proceeds to cast the Spell, using the candles, incenses, oils, poppets, tag-locks etc., as each Spell would call for. (See Spells in previous sections).

***

TO RAISE THE POWER

When the Second Witch has performed the actual working of the Spell, all would meditate on the reason and idea for the working and join hands around the Altar and begin to move widdershins stepping faster and faster as they all, in unison, chant the incantation used by the Second Witch in the Spell itself. It embodies the idea and reason for the working.

This fast movement around the area of the Spellcasting, draws in power from the nether realms to charge up the idea for the Spell and impregnates the area with that intention and energy.

The atmosphere will feel to take on a sense of Power and build in intensity as the circling continues.

When the three Witches feel they can do no more, they fall to the floor or ground in place around
the Altar and intently concentrate on the Spell being already in affect and as having already begun to happen.

After a few minutes meditation on that point, the three witches get up and join hands once again around the Altar and begin the unwinding of the knot of energy they just created.

This is done by moving deosil around the same area and chanting the name of the Subject or Victim over and over and seeing in the Mind's Eye, the Spell winging off and striking the Subject with a boon, or the Victim with a blast.

The deosil motion will unwind that energy and the Witches will feel the Power drain from the area. That is the sign that all is going according to plan.

After the draining feeling, the Witches calmly come to order around the Circle and the Third Witch may then begin the Closing.

***

THE CLOSING

The Circle was cast with Air (Incense), Fire (Candle) and Blade. It should be closed with the other two complimentary Elements: Blade, Water (Chalice) and Earth (Salt).

It should also move in the opposite direction of the casting, id est, deosil.

The Third Witch takes up the Blade and moves deosil from before the Altar to stand at the North Quarter.

He/She inscribes a Banishing Pentagram in the Air at that point with the Blade and says:

SPACE FOR YOUR NOTES/SPELLS/RITUALS FOR YOUR PERSONAL BOOK OF SHADOWS

HECATE, LADY OF MAGIC POWER
WITHDRAW THY MIGHT FROM THIS BOWER.
SEND ALL FORCES AND PHANTOMS BACK
AND OF THY LOVE, LET THERE BE NO LACK!

He/She moves then deosil to the East inscribing the Banishing Pentagram and repeating the words. That is also done at the South and West. Then he/she moves once again past the North and returns to the Altar and replaces the Blade.

Taking up the Chalice of Water, the Third Witch again moves deosil from the Altar to the North and sprinkles a few drops to that direction and says:

WATERS OF CREATION'S WOMB,
RESTORE THE SILENCE OF THE TOMB.
LET PEACE DWELL HERE!
LET IT BE BOTH FAR AND NEAR.

Returning to the Altar by way of another circumambulation deosil from North to North, and repeating and sprinkling the words at each point, the Chalice is relinquished and the Dish of Salt taken up.

With the Salt, the Third Witch silently snuffs out the candle at the North Quarter by setting the dish on top of the Flame and casting a few grains to that direction. This is repeated again around the Circle deosil until all Four Watchtower Candles are extinguished.

He/She gives a final bow to the North and says:

IT IS FINISHED! CONSUMMATUM EST!

Returning to stand before the Altar with the other two Witches, he/she sets the Dish back in place.

All three Witches then clap the hands thrice to scatter the vibration on the atmosphere.

Then they may leave the Circle Area.

Ritual Tools and equipment may be cleared away and a changing out of robes back to normal attire would be in order.

As can be seen from the format of Casting, doing the Spell and the Closing, each participant has something to contribute to the working. It is a total effort on the part of the Witches working a Coven of Three.

Most of the Spells from preceding pages can be worked out to fit in the part played by the Second Witch. He/She should be the one of the three who has the most experience in Spellcasting and the Art Magical.

The rub is, however, that the Spells call to be repeated over a period of several Days. This entails being dedicated enough in practice of the Arts to continue through to the end. It means the Practitioners must put all other demands on time and attention on hold until the Working has been completed.

Faint hearts and haphazardly attempt bring only sterility of results.

The Ritual Procedure must be rehearsed and known by heart well enough to run smoothly without a hitch. The Casting and Closing should be second nature to all participants.

There is sufficient room for individual group creativity in the chants and Invocations used for the Ritual, however, they should be agreed upon by all, so that harmony and one accord pervade the Working.

Having the Ritual Format down pat and conducting it faithfully and completely each time is discipline of the utmost importance in the Art Magical.

A "Lazy Man's Guide To Mastery" does not exist! Magic is only worked with discipline and dedicated effort. If you are only interested in having the name of Witch, but not sufficiently motivated to BE one, and to DO what is required, you are only deluding yourself.

To KNOW is a potent force, yes! But to DO is more powerful still! Real Witches waste no time with Dabblers, Clowns and the Uncommitted.

MAY THE POWER THAT BIDES IN THE SECRET TIDES BLESS THEE AND ALL THY WORKS.

SPACE FOR YOUR NOTES/SPELLS/RITUALS FOR YOUR PERSONAL BOOK OF SHADOWS

SABBAT CEREMONIES FOR A COVEN OF THREE

First let us draw a distinction between what is a Sabbat and what is an Esbat. There seems to be a blurring of the line of demarcation even among some modern Witch Covens.

An Esbat is a gathering of Witches for both the New and Full Moons. The word itself translates as "to frolic", and was, in olden times, the night Witches gathered monthly, or bi-monthly, to work Spells of Magic.

These Spells were for group or community well-being in order to bring needed increase to flock, field, town, manor or person.

They were also for community and collective and individual protection against enemies and dangers.

Esbats were and are the time Witches apply their own invoked and evoked energies brought to bear on matters at hand.

Sabbats were, and should still be, times of worship for the Old Gods. No Magics ought to be conducted on a Sabbat. It is a Holy Day, sacred to the God/Goddess. It is a time to commune with that mighty power, not a time to use one's own energies and conjured Magics.

There are two cycles of Sabbats that have come to be inter-connected in the modern system.

One was the round of the Solar Sabbats of the Solstices and Equinoxes. They came from a tradition that held a concept of Sky-Father. The Male Potency of Deity was seen to order the Times indicated by the configuration of the Heavens.

The other was the Terrestrial Sabbats of the Seasons, sacred to the concept of the Earth Mother. These are the Cross-Quarter Days. They set the flavor of the Season, responding Six Weeks after a Solstice or Equinox, as the Earth reacts to the changes in the Heavens.

Thus they run masculine-feminine alternating around the cycle of the year, each flowing out of and into its opposite.

The only variables are the Solstices and Equinoxes, which are not always on the same day each year. However, they only variate, back and forth within a space of a few days from year to year.

Therefore, traditional times can be set to observe the Sabbats. Traditionally, the Witches Year begins at Hallowmas, October 31. It is a feminine Sabbat, sacred to the Goddess, commemorating Death.

Death is the first step to life. Energy must be expended before anything can live.

Hallowmas observes the Season of Death with a Dumb Supper to commune with Spirits of friends and relatives who have crossed the veil. Then it looks forward to the New Year with Psychic Prognostications.

Mid-Winter, or Winter Solstice is traditionally celebrated on the 21st of December. It is a commemoration of the turn of the Tide. It is a masculine Sabbat for the God as "Child of Promise" bringing new life with the return of the warmth of the Sun to the Northern Hemisphere.

Candlemas Sabbat falls on February 2nd and is feminine to celebrate the reception of Nature's Womb and the beginning of the Growing Season.

Vernal Equinox is traditionally held on the 21st of March to celebrate the masculine energy of Youth and New Life. A balance of Light and Dark Forces are commemorated with emphasis on the positive waxing power of Nature's Bounty.

Beltane, a Season of the Goddess, observes the good fortune and birthing of life in first bloom. It falls on the old Walpurga's Nacht on April 30. The Maiden aspect of the Goddess is celebrated.

Mid-Summer, or Summer Solstice honors the High Tide of the God's Potency with a fire Ritual. It is the time when positive forces of life are at their most virile. June 21st is the traditional Day.

The High Tide of the Goddess follows next at Lammas, on August 2nd. The first fruits from the fields are blessed and a communion with Her is held to ensure Her Bounty.

The Darker Forces of the waning Year begin to manifest at the Sabbat of Autumnal Equinox. Traditionally September 21st is the day. At this Sabbat the forces are equal with the Dark on the wax. A communion of

SPACE FOR YOUR NOTES/SPELLS/RITUALS FOR YOUR PERSONAL BOOK OF SHADOWS

reaping one's dues in life is the theme. It is the Cosmic Justice of the God's Power.

Thus the cycle runs male-female all around the year.

The Sabbats are stepping stones as we tred our way through life, where we can rest and refresh our inner beings in communion with the Heavenly Father God and the Bounteous Earth Mother. From them we can draw sustenance for the Soul. They truly are the Holy Days and should be kept with a religious dedication to the Powers they celebrate.

The cyclic flow of life as seen in the Wisdom of the Old Religion gives Witches a universal outlook. They know that everything comes around again, but on a more progressive level. It affirms the philosophy of Reincarnation and the Law of Compensation (Karma).

The Universe is seen as a Spiral evolving ever onward to perfection as visioned by the Creator; God/Goddess. Everything happens as it should for the ultimate good of all.

This has put the Old Religion into conflict with the Theology of Judaeo-Christianity, which sees History as lineal, having a beginning, a middle and an end, with a definite reward for those who are acceptable to the Christian God.

If it were widely known, we have eons of time to perfect ourselves, in the image of our God/Goddess, the political powers of Clergies would be shown up for what they are: Mind and Thought Control!

That is mainly the reason the Ancient Wisdom Religion was rooted out of the hearts and minds of Western Man in the History of this World.

Be that as it may, Witches still keep the times and observe the Seasons as did the Ancient Wise Ones of Old.

***

THE SABBAT ROUND FOR A COVEN OF THREE

A small Coven of three persons, as described in the preceding pages, would use that Ritual Format for Esbat Ceremonies and at other times to work Magics and cast Spells.

Sabbats, being days of Worship, would have a different program. Because no Magics are worked at and on a Sabbat, and the Coven comes before the God/Goddess to commune and refresh the Soul, a Magic Circle would not be erected as for Spellcraft.

Strong Psychic Barriers to contain Power, Raise the Cone and send the Fetch, as the old words indicate, are not necessary for Sabbat Rituals.

The three Witches holding hands around the Altar, in an act of communion and devotion, create their own simple Psychic Circle, sufficient for worship.

In the center space of the Altar would be the candles and symbols to dedicate and use in the ceremony, as each Sabbat Format, to follow, will indicate.

Due to the fact a Coven of three is composed of experienced Witches, duly initiated into the Craft, no hierarchy has been set up. The group itself may appoint one to act as High Priest or High Priestess and be the Officiant for the Ceremony, or it can have that office alternate among them, as they wish.

A Coven of three is egalitarian and avoids the ego status of a High Priesthood structure, common in larger Covens and Occult Groups. Big frogs in little ponds only make themselves a laughing stock.

It would be best to have the responsibility of the Officiant alternate back and forth among the group, so that each Witch gains experience in handling a Worship Ceremony.

However the group may decide, the Sabbat Rituals must be rehearsed and known sufficiently by heart to be able to roll smoothly, once begun. Lack of preparation reduces a serious Ritual to the level of very amateur theatrics and does not honor the Old Gods.

Observing the Sabbats and engaging in acts of worship to the Old Gods, in communion with the Natural Forces as the Tides and Seasons change, lend a valuable upliftment to the study and use of Occultism.

To engage in Spellcraft without the

SPACE FOR YOUR NOTES/SPELLS/RITUALS FOR YOUR PERSONAL BOOK OF SHADOWS

devotion to the Old Gods, makes one a simple Sorcerer, but not of the Old Religion.

The Round of the Sabbats and the worship of the Old Gods bear an ethical and moral responsibility, which gives the Practitioner a solid foundation and a cause for belief. Sabbats offer us an opportunity to strive ever to better ourselves as Human Beings in Progressive Spiritual Evolution.

With those few remarks out of the way, let us now proceed to the Eight Sabbats of the Year:

SPACE FOR YOUR NOTES/SPELLS/RITUALS FOR YOUR PERSONAL BOOK OF SHADOWS

HALLOWMAS SABBAT--THE HIGH HOLY DAY

WITCHES NEW YEAR

At the Midnight Hour, on the 31st of October, leading into the Day of All Souls, November 1, witches gather to honor the Spirits of those whom they have known and loved, who have crossed the veil and now rest in the Beauty of the Goddess.

This being the most sacred of all Sabbats, it behooves the Officiant to plan and arrange and prepare this ceremony with utmost care.

He/She receives from the other two participants the names of the Spirits of their departed friend or relative with whom they would like to commune, at least two weeks prior to this night.

The Officiant conducts a nightly meditation on the Spirits calling the names of those for the other two witches and for the Spirit who is to commune with him/her self. The two week meditation should be done on the thirteen nights prior to Hallowmas and culminating at the Dumb Supper Ceremony on Sabbat.

That has helped open a channel to the Spirit Realm, so that on Hallowmas it would be easier for the Coven to get a response from the Spirits. This period of private meditation on the part of the Officiant must not be neglected, nor ignored. No Witch, Magician, Wizard or Magus can dispense with preparation time for Occult Rituals, no matter how adept they claim to be. (On the other hand some "Magickians" feel they are above all that!)

On the Night of Hallowmas, the Officiant should be secluded shortly prior to the ceremony to complete the meditation and get in the right frame of mind.

In the meantime, the other two participants prepare the Altar and work area thus:

The Altar is set as usual (see diagram of Magic Circle). In the center space should rest a representation of a Skull and Cross-Bones, either real or imitation.

Flanking that a black and an orange candle.

The Incense for the Rite should be Patchouli, Storax and Benzoin to burn on coals and make thick smoke.

Laid before the skull on the Altar would be a list of the names of the three Spirits who will be summoned during the Ritual and a willow Wand to command the forces.

A hand bell would rest near the list of names.

About five feet away, in front of the Altar a cloth is spread upon the floor and six place settings spread out upon it: plates, knives, forks, spoons, cups and napkins.

At each plate would also be a name card for the living participants and a name card for the Spirit each person invites at the place directly across from him/her.

Upon each plate would be a symbolic meal to share with the Spirits. An unleavened bread, a spicy sweet, nuts, dates and sliced apples.

A sharp cider would be the beverage. However, any seasonal foods and beverages indicative of the Intention of the Rite could be used at the group's discretion. (Pita bread and bitter endive, for example).

The participants would thus sit cross-legged on the floor, directly opposite the Spirit Guest each has called.

All should be prepared and ready, so that at the stroke of the Midnight Hour, the Officiant can begin the Ceremony.

The three Witches, robed and silent, step up to the Altar with the Officiant facing North across it and the other two standing at the East and West respectively.

They all join hands to form a circle around the Altar.

The Officiant invokes:

IT IS SABBAT! THE HOLY HOUR CHIMES.
LET US KEEP THE SEASON AND MARK THE TIMES.
GODDESS OF MYSTERY, GODDESS OF DEATH, GODDESS OF GOOD, GODDESS OF LIFE,
BE WITH US NOW! THE TIME IS RIFE.

SPACE FOR YOUR NOTES/SPELLS/RITUALS FOR YOUR PERSONAL BOOK OF SHADOWS

OPEN THY VEIL BETWEEN THE PLANES
AND SEND AWAY ALL EVIL AND BANES.
TO DUMB SUPPER ON HALLOWMAS NIGHT
SEND THOSE WE CALL WITH LOVE AND LIGHT.

The Officiant lights the two candles flanking the skull and bones from the votive, or Altar Candle, and sets Incense to burn in the Burner.

Taking up the willow Wand, he/she speaks the Necromantic Charge:

BY THE MYSTERY OF NIGHT!
BY THE OLD GODS SACRED LIGHT!
BY THE POWER OF SABBAT RITE!
COME FORTH FROM THE BEYOND!
__________, __________, AND __________
RESPOND, RESPOND FROM THE DEEP BEYOND!

(With the Wand the Altar is tapped at the end of each line)

As each name of a Spirit is said, the Officiant rings the hand bell and then continues:

THROUGH THE FLICKERING CANDLE GLOW
LET THY PRESENCE TO US SHOW.
IN THE INCENSE SMOKE MOST DENSE
THY FORM WE SEE AND SENSE.
COME FORTH FROM THE BEYOND!
COME FORTH AND RESPOND!
BY THE LIVING GODS OF LIFE
THERE IS NO SORROW, LOSS OR STRIFE.
COMMUNE WITH US IN A CIRCLE OF LOVE,
BLESSED BY THE GODDESS FROM ABOVE!

Setting the Wand and bell back upon the Altar, the Officiant joins hands with the other two Participants and all in unison chant:

RED SPIRITS AND WHITE,
BLACK SPIRITS AND GREY,
MINGLE, MINGLE, MINGLE,
YE WHO MINGLE MAY!
AROUND AND AROUND,
THROUGHOUT AND ABOUT,
ALL GOOD COME IN,
ALL ILL KEEP OUT!

Releasing hands, each Witch bows to the North across the Altar.

The Officiant says:

WELCOME, WELCOME IN THE GODDESS'S NAME.
BRING LOVE AND FELLOWSHIP AND WE OFFER YOU SAME.

The two other participants step away from the Altar and sit themselves at the place setting with their name cards directly opposite the Spirit Guest he/she has summoned.

The Officiant takes up the Wand and steps to the side of the place setting where the Spirit Guests are to be seated and taps with the Wand at each place calling out the name of each Spirit to take its seat.

From this point on, all participants maintain strict silence.

The Officiant may place more Incense on the coal in the Burner and take his/her place at the Supper.

The only illumination in the Chamber would be from the three candles on the Altar.

The Incense should begin to fill the area and give an other worldly glow to the Chamber.

Each participant slowly begins to eat his/her meal and silently commune in fellowship with the Spirit Guest seated across the place setting.

Conducted properly, with attention to detail and in a serious frame of mind, a presence of the summoned Spirits will seem to fill the room, and if sufficient energy is put into the meditations, by the living Participants, may even be seen forming as a mist in the swirling smoke.

The Dumb Supper should continue for the better part of the hour.

As the Hour of 1 O'Clock A.M. nears, the power may be felt to wane and the Officiant can get up from the place setting and move to stand behind the places of the Spirit Guests.

He/She taps with the Wand at each place, in the reverse order of seating and speaks each Spirit's name aloud.

All three then get up from the Supper spread and return to the Altar with the

SPACE FOR YOUR NOTES/SPELLS/RITUALS FOR YOUR PERSONAL BOOK OF SHADOWS

Officiant facing North flanked by the other two.

The Officiant says:

RETURN, RETURN TO SUMMERLAND!
TIME HATH PASSED, THE HOUR DOTH DEMAND.
LET PEACE AND BLESSING GUIDE THY WAY BACK TO THE GODDESS TO REST AND TO STAY.
UNTIL HALLOWMAS NEXT, WITH THE DYING LEAVES OF FALL,
TAKE LOVE AND LIGHT AND RESPOND WHEN WE CALL.
BLESSED BE!

The Officiant takes up the hand bell and rings it thirteen times to clear the air and change the vibrations on the Ether.

All three Witches then exclaim:

CONSUMMATUM EST!

The Ritual is over and the items used in it should be cleared away. Left over food (that from the Spirit side) should be silently buried in the Earth the next morning.

The group could give Psychic Readings to each other to see what the Year ahead may hold for each.

Hallowmas Sabbat has been kept.

***

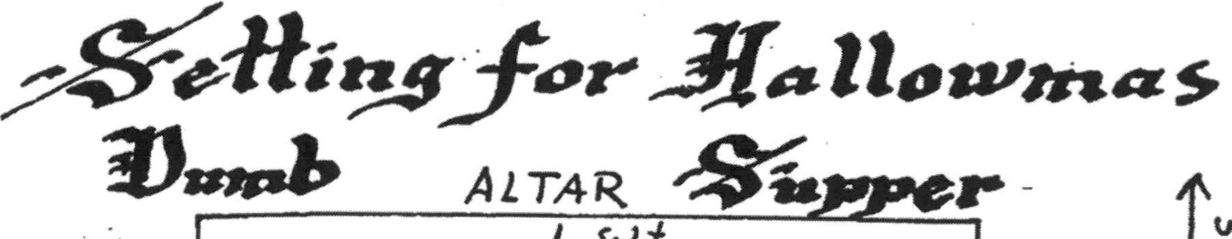

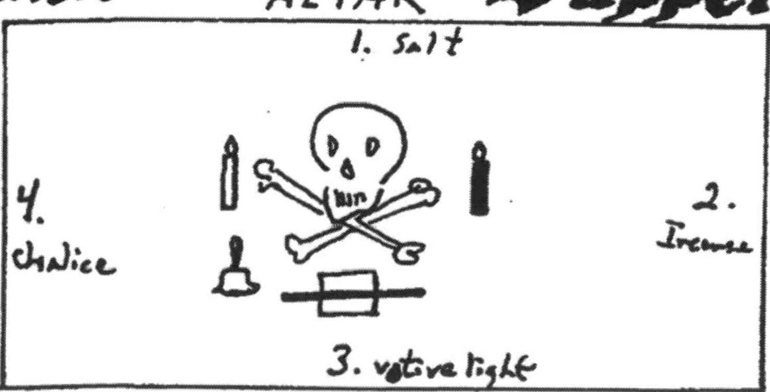

5 feet

SPIRIT GUESTS

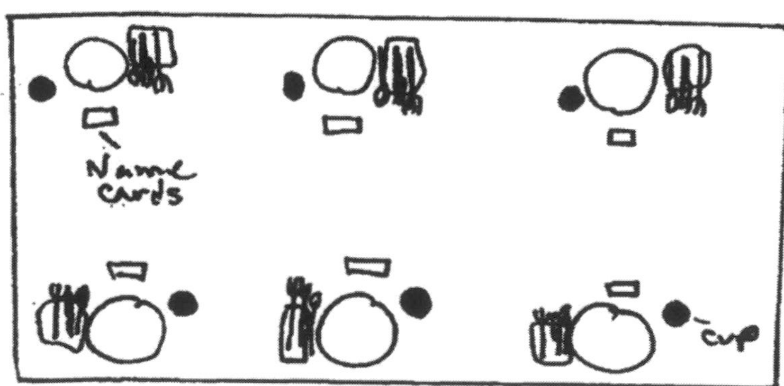

Place setting on The floor

Officiant

LIVING PARTICIPANTS

SPACE FOR YOUR NOTES/SPELLS/RITUALS FOR YOUR PERSONAL BOOK OF SHADOWS

Cauldron Rite
for
Midwinter
c

SPACE FOR YOUR NOTES/SPELLS/RITUALS FOR YOUR PERSONAL BOOK OF SHADOWS

MIDWINTER SABBAT

Hallowmas was celebrated with very serious intent to commemorate the Season of Death. This Sabbat should be somewhat the opposite with rejoicing and good cheer.

In Olden Times it was held, even by Christians, with a "Lord of Misrule" in the Midwinter Revels for buffoonery and practical jokes.

Midwinter celebrated the Turn of the Tide from the depth of the Cold Season to a Return of the Sun and the coming of Spring.

In the Myth of the Old Ways, it is the Day of Winter Solstice, when the Sun begins to appear climbing higher and higher in the Heavens, bringing Life back to the Northern Hemisphere. The Ancient God of Life is said to be reborn at this time. Sabbat celebrates the spark of Life moving in the Womb of Nature.

The Coven of Three could hold Midwinter Sabbat and celebrate this theme very easily. What would be needed can be obtained with a minimum of effort.

A cauldron filled with Earth to stand in the center of the Altar. One large Jumbo sized Red Candle to stand in the center of the cauldron in the earth. One small red candle for each participant.

On the Altar, the cauldron would be draped and rung with seasonal plants such as Holly, Pine Sprigs and Cones and seasonal red flowers.

The Incense should be Pine and an anointing oil of Cinnamon would add to the scent.

An item indicative of the Earth Fire would also be needed. Tradition says the Spark of Life from the womb of Nature should be obtained.

That means Flint and Steel. (A modern cigarette lighter.)

Three days prior to Sabbat, the Altar and Chamber should be cleaned and stripped down to bareness. No lights should be in the Ritual Chamber and all left to sit in cold, silence and darkness.

On the Day of Midwinter, the Altar and Chamber are re-dressed with clean equipment.

The Altar Cloth should be black and the cleaned Altar Tools reset.

No votive light would be lit.

The items for the ceremony would rest in the center space awaiting the Ceremony later at night.

At the time for Sabbat, the three Witches approach the darkened Altar in silence. This is the height of the Rule of Winter. Robed and hooded, the Witches commune with this dark and heavy time.

The officiant takes up the Flint and Steel and says:

OLD GODS OF OUR ANCIENT FAITH HEAR US!
OUT OF THE DEPTHS OF THIS NIGHT OF TIME, WE CALL UNTO THEE!
LET CRUEL WINTER'S REIGN BE PUT ON THE WANE!

All three chime in unison:

SEND TO US THE CHILD OF PROMISE! IO EHVOE HE! THE LORD OF LIFE IS BORN THIS DAY!

The Officiant produces a spark from the Flint and Steel and puts it out. The three Witches repeat the call and a second spark is produced and put out. The third time the call is given the Officiant produces the spark and lights the candle in the center of the cauldron. All chime together:

SEE THE YOUNG LORD BORN THIS NIGHT!
OLD MAN WINTER IS PUT TO FLIGHT!
BLESSED BE AND BLESSED BE!

The Officiant then lights the votive candle in space #3 and the coal to burn Incense. Some Incense is placed upon the coal and the Flint and Steel are laid aside.

The Officiant says:

BY THE TURNING OF THE TIDE,
BRING JOY AND LAUGHTER TO OUR SIDE!
THE GREAT MOTHER KEEPS OUR LIFE WITHIN HER WOMB.
SHE OFFERS LIFE AND BELIES THE TOMB!
RAISE THE POWER OF THE GOD OF LIGHT
REACHING UPWARD IN JOY AND MIGHT!

SPACE FOR YOUR NOTES/SPELLS/RITUALS FOR YOUR PERSONAL BOOK OF SHADOWS

All three join hands around the Altar and begin to move widdershins around and around, faster and faster to draw in the Power.
As they move, they all chant together:

LORD OF LIFE, WE CALL TO THEE!
LET THE REIGN OF GOODNESS BE!
DRAW IN TO US BY ANCIENT RITE
AND LIVE WITHIN OUR INNER SIGHT!
WARM US, HEAL US, BRING US JOY!
THOU ART THE LADY'S NEW BORN BOY!
THE THRALL OF DEATH BE BROKEN NOW,
SOON THE EARTH WILL FEEL THE PLOW.
LIFE COMES BACK TO HEARTH AND HOME
BORN ON THE SEA IN SPRAY AND FOAM.
GIVE LIFE! GIVE LIFE! GIVE JOY AND LOVE!
WE SEEK THY BLESSINGS FROM ABOVE!

The circling and chanting should continue until the Officiant feels enough power and energy has been drawn into the Circle area. He/She stops and says:

GOOD WITCHES ALL, THIS YULETIDE TIME, COMMUNE WITH HIM AND LET HEARTS UPWARD CLIMB.

He/She takes up the three small red candles and gives one to each of the other two participants.

Then each is given a dab of the anointing oil.

All three witches then dress his/her individual candle with whatever personal wish and desire each would have to bring before the God. In silence each anoints his/her own candle and communes with the Lord of Life in Spirit.

Then each Witch lights his/her candle from the large one on the Altar in the cauldron, and places it to stand in the Earth next to the large one. In the depths of being, each Witch prays for the personal petition before the God of Life.

The Officiant then says:

WE THANK THEE, OUR ANCIENT GODS, FOR THIS TIME OF JOY. GRANT US THE FULFILLMENT OF OUR DESIRES AS MAY BE MOST EXPEDIENT FOR US. WE ACCEPT THY ANCIENT WISDOM AS THY DUTIFUL CHILDREN. BLESSED BE!

Consummatum Est!

The candles are left to burn out and the Witches may depart the area.

A holiday dinner with Old World cuisine may be celebrated and much joking and good cheer as the group would like, should continue from then throughout the night.

With the Dawn, the Witches should go out and greet the New Born Sun.

The Spirit of the Sabbat Has Been Kept.

Witch and wizard riding to the Sabbath.

SPACE FOR YOUR NOTES/SPELLS/RITUALS FOR YOUR PERSONAL BOOK OF SHADOWS

Cauldron Rite
for
Candlemas

SPACE FOR YOUR NOTES/SPELLS/RITUALS FOR YOUR PERSONAL BOOK OF SHADOWS

CANDLEMAS SABBAT

Candlemas follows six Weeks later from the Winter Solstice and celebrates the Seasonal change as the Earth reacts to the Solar Tide. As Midwinter commemorated the Return of the Solar Energy, Candlemas celebrates the Preparation of the Earth for Planting.

According to the Myth, The Earth Mother's Womb must be made receptive to the seed and the rain.

The item needed for this Sabbat would primarily be a large Jumbo-sized Black Candle. It represents the Light coming from Darkness. It is the sprout of the Seed growing from Nature's earthy sleep.

To that would be added three smaller black candles for the three participants and three squares of parchment, upon which each has written a petition of good resolve; something needed and wanted to bring to flower in the individual's life.

An Incense of earthy scent such as Sweet Grass or Sandalwood, and an anointing oil of Verbena.

The cauldron, in the center of the Altar would be empty and beside it would rest seeds and bulbs to be planted in the Earth after Sabbat.

the Chalice in space #4, on the Altar, filled with water, would be used in the Libation of the Earth when planting the seeds and bulbs.

Each Witch writes a clear petition of something personal that he/she hopes to bring about in his/her life and resolves to do what would be necessary to bring it to flower. The petitions are carried tucked into the cinch cord around the waist, when robed and ready for Sabbat.

The Altar is set and the votive in space #3 burning. All items mentioned above rest in place upon it.

The Witches approach the Altar with the Officiant leading. Taking places and joining hands around the Altar a moment of silence is observed to first link up with the idea of the Goddess for this ceremony.

The Officiant says:

IT IS SABBAT. THE HOLY HOUR HAS STRUCK. BEHOLD, BEFORE US THE MYSTIC WOMB OF THE GODDESS - THE CAULDRON OF LIFE ETERNAL.
THE LADY STIRS AND AWAKENS FROM THE SLUMBER OF WINTER. DEEP WITHIN THE DARKNESS OF EARTH THE SEED OF LIFE WILL SPROUT.
LET US PREPARE THE GODDESS TO BRING FORTH THE MIRACLE OF LIFE.
BLESSED BE!

Taking the votive candle, the Officiant lights the large black one standing beside the cauldron and says:

THY LIGHT, LADY, I NOW CALL FORTH! LET IT WAX AND FILL THIS WORLD OF FORM.
BE THY LIGHT, LADY, MY STEPS ARE LED. BY THY LIFE, O GODDESS, MY DAYS ARE MEASURED.

Lighting some Incense he/she continues:

LET THE SWEET EARTHY SCENT OF LIFE GIVE ESSENCE AND STRENGTH TO OUR WORKS OF SABBAT.
AS THE LADY BRINGS FORTH THE BUD, LET US MANIFEST OUR RESOLVES INN LIFE.

Joining hands each Witch begins to circle the Altar moving widdershins as all chant:

COME, O, WAXING LIGHT OF LIFE!
COME, O, GENTLE RAINS OF SPRING!
COME, O, SPROUT OF SEED!
BRING TO US ACCOMPLISHED DEED!

The Officiant continues the circling and chanting until it is felt sufficient power has been raised. He/She calls the group to order and says:

GOOD WITCHES ALL, LET US GIVE OUR RESOLVES TO HER. THAT SHE MAY WORK THE MIRACLE OF LIFE!

SPACE FOR YOUR NOTES/SPELLS/RITUALS
FOR YOUR PERSONAL BOOK OF SHADOWS

The Officiant hands each Witch a small black candle and places a dab of the Verbena Oil in each one's hands.

All participants silently dress his/her own candle with the oil and communes with the Goddess praying for the fulfillment of the private written petition.

When each candle is dressed, it is lit from the large black one and set to burn with a written petition beneath it.

The Officiant then says:

LET US LAY THE SEED OF LIFE AND THE SEED OF DEED INTO THE LADY'S WOMB.

The seeds and bulbs are placed in the bottom of the cauldron and the written petitions are placed beside them.

Then the large candle, in a holder is set to stand and burn inside the cauldron.

The Officiant says:

THE WORK IS DONE! THE LADY OF LIFE DOTH CONCEIVE ANEW!
Consummatum Est!

The Witches may retire from the Altar and enjoy a Sabbat Supper of herbs and spice and fresh bread and cheese with cider.

After the communion Supper, the Witches take the cauldron, the large candle and the Chalice of water out of doors.

One of the participants digs a hole in the earth with a wooden spoon, or sharp digging stick, to the shape of a furrow.

The Officiant places the seeds, bulbs and petitions into the furrow from out of the cauldron, buries them with earth and places the candle stub to stand at the spot.

The third Witch pours water from the Chalice onto the spot as the Officiant says:

LADY, ACCEPT OUR ACT OF LOVE! LET RAIN AND SUN BRING FORTH THY LIFE! BE EVER RENEWED AND REFRESHED AND BRING FORTH THE BUD, AS WE STRIVE TO BRING FORTH GOOD DEED. BLESSED BE!

The Witches may repair indoors and clear the Sabbat tools away.

THE SPIRIT OF THE SABBAT HAS BEEN KEPT.

The three black candles lit by each participant should be put out after the burial of the seeds and taken home by each one to be burned for good luck at a convenient time during the following week.

THE ART OF ALCHEMY

SPACE FOR YOUR NOTES/SPELLS/RITUALS FOR YOUR PERSONAL BOOK OF SHADOWS

Vernal
Equinox

SPACE FOR YOUR NOTES/SPELLS/RITUALS FOR YOUR PERSONAL BOOK OF SHADOWS

VERNAL EQUINOX

This is the Tide of new beginnings, when life affirms itself in the new growth of Spring. Light and dark are equal with the bright tide on the wax.

Traditionally, Witches re-affirm their commitment to the Old Religion and to the Ancient Wisdom at this time. Renewal is the theme.

The Altar would be set with its usual equipment and in the center space would sit a large Pentagram, symbol of the Faith, flanked by a white and black candle to show the balance of the Forces.

The Incense would be herbal, grassy or floral, such as Mint, Verbena or Jasmine.

An Anointing Oil of Rosemary and Verbena, or perhaps Lemon or Citrus would be the Sabbat Oil.

(Usually, for Esbats and works of ordinary Spellcraft the Altar drape would be purple. For Sabbats, however, any color indicative of the Time or Season could be used.)

At the time for the ceremony, the three Witches approach the Altar and join hands around it.

The Officiant says:

THE EQUINOX OF SPRING IS UPON US, IT IS SABBAT, THE HOLY DAY OF NEW BEGINNINGS AND THE RE-AFFIRMATION OF LIFE.
WE CALL UPON THE GOD OF LIGHT AND SEEK TO BALANCE IN OURSELVES THE HARMONY OF LOVE AND LIFE. BLESSED BE!

Taking up the votive candle from the Altar, the Officiant lights the white and black candle flanking the Pentagram, sets the votive back in place and places some Incense to burn, says:

LIGHT AND DARK STAND EQUAL IN TIME WITH THE GROWING LIGHT OF LOVE BEING PRIME.
AS GREEN GROWS THE SPROUT ABOVE GROUND,
LET US RE-AFFIRM OUR WISDOM PROFOUND.

Joining hands once again, all three Witches chant the Litany of the Pentagram and the Tenets of the Faith, meditating on the Pentagram:

I SEE THE SYMBOL OF MY GOD AND GODDESS.
BE THEY BLESSED FOREVER AND A DAY.
I SEE THE OLD RELIGION'S SIGN AND COVENANT.
BE IT BLESSED FOREVER AND A DAY.
I SEE THE ANCIENT WISDOM TRUE.
CONFIRMED IN ME FOREVER AND A DAY.
THE TOPMOST POINT IS THE FIRE OF SPIRIT ANIMATING THE PLANE OF MATTER.
SO SAY THE ANCIENT WISE ONES FROM OF OLD.
THE LOWER LEFT POINT SAYS TO WALK IN BALANCE ALL MY DAYS,
NOTHING TOO MUCH AND NOTHING TOO LITTLE,
NOTHING TOO GOOD AND NOTHING TOO BAD,
I AVOID EXCESS AND ALL EXTREMES.
SO SAY THE ANCIENT WISE ONES FROM OF OLD.
THE UPPER RIGHT POINT TELLS ME TO BE IN HARMONY WITH ALL DAME NATURE'S CREATED BEINGS, THE MINERALS, THE PLANTS, THE ANIMALS AND MY FELLOW MAN.
SO SAY THE ANCIENT WISE ONES FROM OF OLD.
THE UPPER LEFT POINT SPEAKS TO ME OF PERFECT LOVE AND PERFECT TRUST.
LOVE SEEKS THE BEST FOR ALL MY FELLOWS AND CLINGS NOT.
TRUST KNOWS THAT ALL THINGS HAPPEN FOR THE ULTIMATE GOOD IN THE GODS UNFOLDING PLAN.
SO SAY THE ANCIENT WISE ONES FROM OF OLD.
THE LOWER RIGHT POINT TELLS ME OF THE TIMES BEFORE,
AND OF THE TIMES THAT WILL BE AGAIN.
THIS WORLD I'VE KNOWN IN AGES PAST, I KNOW IT NOW, AND WILL RETURN AGAIN.
EACH LIFE CYCLE LEADS ME EVER UPWARD INTO THE GODS PERFECTED STATES OF BEING.

SPACE FOR YOUR NOTES/SPELLS/RITUALS FOR YOUR PERSONAL BOOK OF SHADOWS

SO SAY THE ANCIENT WISE ONES FROM OF OLD.
AS I BEAR THE SYMBOL OF MY FAITH, LET IT BURN DEEP WITHIN MY SOUL AND CONFIRM IN ME THE OLD GODS LOVE.
BLESSED BE THE ANCIENT WISDOM.

The Officiant takes a dab of the Anointing Oil and anoints, with the thumb, a Pentagram upon the forehead of the other two participants and then anoints him/her self.

The three together, chant:

I BELIEVE IN THE SUPREME BEING KNOWN TO MANKIND AS THE GOD AND GODDESS, CO-EQUAL AND CO-ETERNAL.
I BELIEVE IN HONORING THE GODS AT THE EIGHT SABBATS OF THE YEARLY ROUND.
I BELIEVE THE HUMAN MIND IS THE GREATEST GIFT OF THE GODS. IT WILL LEAD MANKIND EVER FORWARD TO PERCEIVE THE DIVINE ESSENCE IN ALL LIVING BEINGS.
I BELIEVE IN OBSERVING DISCRETION IN ALL MATTERS PERTAINING TO THE CRAFT COMMUNICATED TO THE STRANGER.
I BELIEVE IN ESTABLISHING WITHIN MYSELF A BALANCED LIFE IN HARMONY WITH ALL OTHER PARTS OF THE MANIFESTED UNIVERSE.
I BELIEVE THAT NOTHING IN NATURE IS UGLY OR UNHOLY.
I BELIEVE IN PERFECT LOVE AND PERFECT TRUST, TEMPERED TO THOSE OF GOOD WILL AND WORTHY.
I BELIEVE IN WALKING IN HUMILITY WITH MY GODS AND IN MY RELATIONSHIPS WITH ALL MY FELLOW BEINGS.
I BELIEVE IN BEING PATIENT WITH AND IN GIVING UNDERSTANDING TO THOSE LESS EVOLVED ON LIFE'S PATH.
I BELIEVE LIVING IS AN ETERNAL PROCESS OF LEARNING.
I BELIEVE IN THE PROGRESSIVE SPIRITUAL EVOLUTION OF THE HUMAN SOUL-THROUGH THE PROCESS OF SUCCESSIVE LIFE CYCLES ON EARTH AND ON SPIRITUAL PLANES.
I BELIEVE IN CAUSE AND EFFECT AND ACCEPT ALL ESOTERIC RELIGIONS AS SISTER FAITHS TO WICCA.
I BELIEVE IN HOLDING MY THOUGHTS STEADFAST FOR THE GOOD, THAT I MAY EXPERIENCE ONLY GOOD IN THE INTERIMS BETWEEN INCARNATIONS.
BLESSED BE THE ANCIENT WISDOM!

After a few moments meditation on the meaning of the recited words, the Officiant then says:

GOOD WITCHES ALL, LET US GO FORTH AND SHOW OUR LIGHT BEFORE THE WORLD.
MAY THE BLESSINGS OF THE GOD OF LIGHT GUIDE OUR PATH FOREVER.
BLESSED BE!
Consummatum Est!

The three Witches retire from the area, leaving the candles to burn themselves out.

SABBAT HAS BEEN KEPT.

SPACE FOR YOUR NOTES/SPELLS/RITUALS FOR YOUR PERSONAL BOOK OF SHADOWS

Beltane Sabbat

SPACE FOR YOUR NOTES/SPELLS/RITUALS FOR YOUR PERSONAL BOOK OF SHADOWS

BELTANE SABBAT

Since Time Immemorial the ancient Fertility Cult has celebrated May Eve as a Season of Communion with the Maiden aspect of the Goddess.

As the Vernal Equinox commemorates the growing power of the God, Beltane is the seasonal response of the Goddess in showing growing things in bloom and the birthing of new life. Spring is at its height.

Large Covens may observe this Sabbat with Fire Leaping or by dancing a May Pole. A smaller coven of three, such as outlined in this tome, would celebrate with a less elaborate ceremony.

Beltane stands directly across the Year from Hallowmas and should be a time of joy and happiness at the prospect of life, in the here and now. Nothing indicative of Death should be displayed nor thought upon.

The cauldron should be set to overflowing with seasonal flowers. There should be pink candles for all participants to dress and dedicate to the Goddess.

An Incense of floral scent such as Rose, Lavender or Cherry Blossom would be appropriate.

An Anointing Oil of Jasmine, Lotus or Gardenia would also be in keeping with the theme.

The Chalice would hold a light rose wine and stand before the flowers in the cauldron.

The planted thoughts, put into the ground at Candlemas, should be being nurtured along by the efforts of each Witch. There should be some indication as to how the resolves are manifesting. Beltane is to re-enforce them along.

At the time for Sabbat the three Witches stand at the Altar with joined hands to create a circle.

The Officiant says:

IT IS SABBAT. MAY THE JOYOUS BLESSINGS OF THE LADY'S SEASON BE WITH US ALL. BLESSED BE!

Lighting the Incense from the votive candle, the Officiant continues:

GODDESS OF THE SPRINGTIME FLOWER,
LET BLESSING AND LIFE UPON US SHOWER.
COME TO THIS CIRCLE SO ROUND
AND LET THY JOY SPREAD AND ABOUND.

Still holding the votive candle, the Officiant says:

AS LAMB AND BIRD GIVE BIRTH IN SPRING
LET OUR VOICES TO THEE SING.
(All join in)
MAIDEN OF THE SPRINGTIME FAIR,
WITH JOY AND MIRTH AND FLOWING HAIR,
COMMUNE WITH US THIS SACRED DAY
AND LET THY LIFE WITH US STAY.

(The votive is replaced on the Altar)
Then the Officiant continues alone:

WE SEEK THY POWER ON OUR WORK, O LADY OF LIFE.
BLESS OUR EFFORTS AND KEEP AWAY STRIFE.
ACCEPT OUR THOUGHTS WE SEND TO THEE.
MANIFEST OUR WISHES AND LET THEM BE!

The Officiant hands each participant a pink candle and gives each a dab of the oil.

All three Witches silently dress and charge the candle to be the intention of re-enforcing the petition planted at Candlemas.

If such has already manifested in a Witch's life, this could be a dedication for thanksgiving.

When all three pink candles have been charged, each one lights it from the votive and places it to stand on the Altar.

Taking up the Chalice of wine, the Officiant proceeds out of the Chamber, and out of doors, followed by the others.

Out under Sky, he/she dedicates the Libation thus:

BLESSED GODDESS OF LIFE ETERNAL.
WE GIVE TO THEE ALL THAT WE ARE.
ACCEPT OUR LIBATION TO THY POTENT MIGHT
AND KEEP US ON THY PATH OF RIGHT.
BLESSED BE!

SPACE FOR YOUR NOTES/SPELLS/RITUALS FOR YOUR PERSONAL BOOK OF SHADOWS

The Officiant gives each participant a sip of the wine from the Chalice and sips him/her self.

Then silently the remaining wine is poured onto the ground, a few drops at a time, deosil: East, South, West and North.

As the wine is libated, each Witch sends a silent blessing with it to all Quarters of the World where the Lady's Love is needed.

The Officiant then proceeds back to the Ritual Chamber and replaces the Chalice. All three gather again around the Altar and recite:

GODDESS OF THIS WORLD'S WIDE RIM,
FILL IT WITH LOVE TO THE BRIM.
WINE AND ROSES, THIS SABBAT DOTH ENTAIL.
FOREVER LET IT OUR GRACIOUS GODDESS HAIL!
BLESSED BE AND BLESSED BE!

The candles are left to burn themselves out.

Each Witch may then go a-Maying as he/she sees fit.

THE SPIRIT OF THE SABBAT HAS BEEN KEPT.

SPACE FOR YOUR NOTES/SPELLS/RITUALS FOR YOUR PERSONAL BOOK OF SHADOWS

Midsummer

SPACE FOR YOUR NOTES/SPELLS/RITUALS FOR YOUR PERSONAL BOOK OF SHADOWS

MIDSUMMER SABBAT

The Summer Solstice Sabbat celebrates the High Point of the Solar Tide to commune with the God as Power and Might. It is a Fire Ritual to bless and ritualistically cleanse the Coven's Ritual Chamber with the Fire drawn from the Sun.

A large red candle, three small white ones and a Chalice of rich red Wine would be the main ingredients needed.

A magnifying glass or lens with some saltpetre, wood shavings, dry grass, Frankincense and charcoal would also be needed.

An Anointing Oil of Frankincense along with a Hand Bell would rest upon the Altar with the candles.

Prior to the actual Sabbat, the Coven takes the Incense Burner with the lens and the saltpetre mixed with the wood shavings and dry grass and the charcoal out under the sun.

The Officiant will draw down the Sun by focusing the rays of Sunlight onto the mixture on the charcoal, to produce a flame. One of the other two Witches will carry the large red candle and light it from the flame produced. The third Witch will then gather up the Burner and return it to the Altar in the Ritual Chamber.

The new flame, on the large red candle is handed to the Officiant so the Sabbat can begin.

Standing outside the Ritual Chamber, holding the New Fire, the Officiant says:

IT IS SABBAT. LET ALL EVIL AND NEGATIVE THINGS FLEE BEFORE THE GOD OF LIGHT. LET THIS TEMPLE BE CLEANSED BY THE GOOD GOD'S MIGHT!

The three Witches proceed into the Ritual Chamber following the candle and come to stand around the Altar. The Officiant places the New Fire in the center on the Altar.

A few grains of Frankincense are placed on the burning charcoal as he/she continues:

GOD OF UNIVERSES, GOD OF LIGHT, ATTEND TO US DURING SABBAT RITE. CLEANSE THIS TEMPLE AND BLESS OUR LIVES, AS WE DEDICATE OURSELVES TO THEE!

Joining hands, the three Witches begin to circle the Altar moving widdershins and chanting in unison:

MAY THE GOOD GOD BLESS THIS COVEN!
MAY POWER AND MIGHT DRIVE ALL EVIL AWAY!
MAY ALL OUR EFFORTS BE BLESSED WITH SUCCESS!
MAY JOY AND LIFE BE REFLECTED THIS SABBAT DAY!

The circling and chanting should continue until the Officiant feels sufficient power has been drawn into the Circle area.

He/She brings all to order and says:

GOOD WITCHES ALL, BRING YOUR PERSONAL NEEDS BEFORE THE GOD OF LIGHT. COMMUNE WITH HIM IN STRENGTH AND JOY. SEE HIM IN THE NEW FIRE AT THIS SABBAT ALTAR. BLESSED BE!

He/She gives a white candle to each participant and takes one him/her self. Placing a bit of the oil on the strongest hand of each participant, he/she says:

GOOD WITCHES, DRESS THIS CANDLE FOR YOURSELF AND ASK WHATEVER BLESSING YOU WOULD NEED OF HIM.

Each participant then communes in silence dressing the candle as a Petition and lighting it from the flame of the large red candle.

When all three white candles have been lit and placed upon the Altar, the Officiant takes up the Chalice of red Wine and gives each other participant and him/her self to sip and says:

MAY THE GOD OF LIGHT AND LOVE AND LIFE BLESS THEE AND ALL THY WORKS! BLESSED BE AND BLESSED BE!

SPACE FOR YOUR NOTES/SPELLS/RITUALS FOR YOUR PERSONAL BOOK OF SHADOWS

After all have been given to sip, the chalice is replaced upon the Altar and the large red candle taken up by the Officiant. One of the other two takes up the burning incense in its Burner and the third takes up the Hand Bell.

Following the Officiant around the Ritual Chamber and out and around the entire building the candle is carried and a Solar Cross is inscribed in the Air with the Flame of the New Fire in every nook and corner.

The place is also censed and the bell rung six times in each spot.

As the Blessing of Fire is being given, the Officiant chants:

FIRE OF FIRE DRIVE OUT EVIL DESIRE!
FIRE OF FIRE LET NO NEGATIVES CONSPIRE!
FIRE OF FIRE BRING IN ALL GOODNESS AND LIGHT!
FIRE OF FIRE SYMBOL OF OUR GOD OF MIGHT!

After the entire area has been thus blessed the candle, incense and bell are replaced upon the Altar. The Officiant says:

BE THIS SACRED TEMPLE, THIS COVENSTEAD OF THE OLD RELIGION, SECURE AND BLESSED FOR ANOTHER YEAR. LET IT BE A BEACON OF THE OLD WISDOM RELIGION TO SHINE FORTH ITS LIGHT TO ALL THE WORLD.
LET THE SPIRITS BE SUMMONED BY THE BELL!
LET THE LAWS BE TAUGHT BY THE BOOK!
LET THE ANCIENT WISDOM SHINE LIKE THE CANDLE!
THUS FROM OF OLD IT HAS ALWAYS BEEN, THUS IT SHALL EVER BE!
Consummatum Est!

The three Witches may then retire from the area leaving the candles and incense to burn themselves out.

SABBAT HAS BEEN KEPT.

If at all possible, the new Fire should be put upon a glass encased 7 Day candle and kept going until just before Midwinter, when the Fire from the Earth Elements, flint and steel is procured at Midwinter Sabbat.

The Midwinter Fire should also be kept going in the same way until just prior to Midsummer, when the Sun is drawn down.

All candles throughout the year, for Esbat Works, Sabbat Ceremonies and Spellcraft and Coven Magics should be lit from this Sacred Flame. In that way the ancient tradition of a Covenstead's Hearthfire is ritually maintained to symbolize the Spirit of the Craft and Coven.

Should the actual day of Midsummer be overcast, so a New Fire can not be obtained, it is permissible to celebrate on the next sunny day within the octave of the Season; within the next eight days following the actual Sabbat in order to procure an authentic New Fire.

SPACE FOR YOUR NOTES/SPELLS/RITUALS FOR YOUR PERSONAL BOOK OF SHADOWS

Lammas
Sabbat

SPACE FOR YOUR NOTES/SPELLS/RITUALS FOR YOUR PERSONAL BOOK OF SHADOWS

LAMMAS

The Earth's response to the High Point of the God's Power comes six Weeks later with a celebration of the High Point of the Goddess. Lammas is the symbolic blessing of the First Fruits.

The Goddess is thanked for Her Bounty and part of the harvest is ritually given back to Her to ensure Her Fecundity forever.

A Chalice of White Wine, a plate of Home-made Bread are the two main ingredients for Lammas.

A large black candle and a smaller white one to show the waning tide of the Season of Growth would rest on the Altar.

The Incense would be of spice, such as Cinnamon, Clove, Nutmeg, or Allspice.

At the time for Sabbat, the three Witches approach the Altar and join hands around it.

The Officiant says:

IT IS SABBAT! THE HOLY DAY OF THE GODDESS OF LIFE, THE CELEBRATION OF EARTH'S FERTILE BOUNTY IS THIS SACRED SEASON.

The Officiant lights the small white candle from the Altar Candle in space #3 and then the large black one, with these words:

AS THE DAYS SHORTEN AND THE NIGHT OF TIME GROWS STRONG, LET US COMMUNE WITH THE LADY AND GIVE HER JOYOUS THANKS FOR THE LOVE SHE SO RICHLY BESTOWS ON ALL HER CREATION.

The Incense is lit with these words:

THE SCENT OF SPICE AND THE SPICE OF LIFE GIVE FLAVOR TO THIS SACRED RITE. BLESSED BE!

Taking up the plate of bread, the Officiant gives each participant a bit to eat.

When all have consumed the piece of bread, the chalice is passed around for all to sip. (A fair measure must be left in the Chalice.)

When all have been given to drink the Officiant says:

GOOD WITCHES ALL, AS YOU HAVE PARTAKEN SO FREELY OF THE BOUNTY OF THE GODDESS, AS YOU HAVE BEEN NURTURED AND SUSTAINED BY HER LOVE, GIVE EAR TO THIS ANCIENT CUSTOM!
FOR ALL THE FREELY GIVEN SUSTENANCE WE DO HUMBLY GIVE THANKS!
FOR ALL THE PLANTS, FLOWERS AND TREES, WE DO HUMBLY GIVE THANKS!
FOR ALL THE WONDROUS LIFE FORMS OF ANIMAL AND HUMAN, WE DO HUMBLY GIVE THANKS!

The two other participants bend down and rap upon the floor thrice, as the Officiant continues:

LADY OF LIFE, HOLY EARTH MOTHER, SHE OF THE CORN AND FIELD! ACCEPT OUR ANCIENT RITE OF LOVE!

The Witches proceed out of doors following the Officiant carrying the plate of bread and the Chalice of wine.

One of the other two digs a small furrow in the Earth, large enough to contain the loaf of bread.

The Officiant places the bread into the Earth.

The third participant buries the bread with the earth taken from the furrow.

The Officiant then pours the Wine upon the spot and says:

LADY OF LIFE, BE THOU ALWAYS BLESSED! BE THOU FOREVER FERTILE! BE THOU OUR NURTURING MOTHER TO TIME WITHOUT END, BLESSED BE! MAY THY BOUNTY RETURN EVER TO THEE!
MAY THY HUMAN CHILDREN NEVER FORGET THESE THY ANCIENT RITES! MAY THOU ALWAYS BE HONORED AND RESPECTED BY ALL WHO OWE THEIR LIFE TO THEE! BLESSED BE AND BLESSED BE!

The three Witches return to the Ritual Chamber and join hands around the Altar. The Officiant says:

SPACE FOR YOUR NOTES/SPELLS/RITUALS FOR YOUR PERSONAL BOOK OF SHADOWS

WE HAVE KEPT THE LAMMAS RITE. LET US NEVER FORGET OUR GRACIOUS GODDESS OF LIFE AND LOVE!

Consummatum Est!

The Witches may then retire from the area, leaving the incense and candles to burn out.

SABBAT HAS BEEN KEPT.

SPACE FOR YOUR NOTES/SPELLS/RITUALS FOR YOUR PERSONAL BOOK OF SHADOWS

Autumn Equinox

SPACE FOR YOUR NOTES/SPELLS/RITUALS FOR YOUR PERSONAL BOOK OF SHADOWS

AUTUMN EQUINOX

This is the Judgment Hour for the Cycle of the Sabbats. It is the Time Witches look inward and commune with the God as to how each and every one has stacked up on the Cosmic Scale of Compensation. Have the good resolves, planted in the Spring come to fruit? Have the hopes and aspirations been positive? Have negative words, works and attitudes put a blotch upon character?

This is the Sabbat when Witches must face themselves as they are and symbolically eat the fruits of their own making.

Each person must judge him/her self alone before the God and accept responsibility for his/her own actions and works. There is no way to avoid the Cosmic Law of Compensation. We make or unmake ourselves.

That is what the Autumn Equinox teaches.

The balance of the Tide of Light is symbolized by a white and a black candle of the same size.

The Incense would be earthy, such as Patchouli.

On the Altar would sit a basket of Harvest Fruit, plates for each participant and a paring knife for each. An Hour Glass to suggest the passage of Time and a Scales to represent the Compensation and dues of life may also be added as meditative themes.

At the time for the ceremony all Witches approach the Altar, join hands around it as the Officiant says:

THIS IS THE SABBAT OF JUDGMENT. THIS IS THE AWFUL HOUR OF THE GOD!

He/She lights the two candles and sets the Incense to burn with these words:

COMES THE COMPENSATION WE HAVE ACCRUED, COMES THE PAYING OF THE PIPER!
WE ARE WHAT WE ARE, ALONE BEFORE OUR MIGHT GOD.
WOULD WE HAVE ABUNDANCE; DID WE PLANT LOVE?
WOULD WE HAVE LOVE; DID WE PLANT JOY?
WOULD WE HAVE JUSTICE; DID WE PLANT FAIRNESS?
ONLY THE GOD AND OURSELVES KNOW THE INNER DEPTHS OF OUR BEING.
NOW WE MUST FACE HIM AS WE ARE!

All Witches join hands and begin to move widdershins around the Altar, chanting as they go:

COME, LORD OF THE KARMIC SCALE,
COME GOD OF JUSTICE AND RIGHT.
COME TO THIS SABBAT CIRCLE AND COMMUNE WITH US!

The officiant brings the group to order and silently hands each one a plate and a knife and says:

GOOD WITCHES ALL, NOW TAKE THE HARVEST FRUITS OF THINE OWN MAKING AND EAT THY DUE BEFORE OUR LORD OF LIGHT. BLESSED BE!

In silence each Witch sits down before the Altar and consumes the fruit of the year's Harvest from the basket, communing with the God in the inner depths of his/her own being.

The Hour Glass may be set to run as the group communes until the sands of time run out.

The candles are left to burn away and each Witch may depart fortified by individual communion with the God.

SABBAT HAS BEEN KEPT.

THE CYCLE IS COMPLETE

SPACE FOR YOUR NOTES/SPELLS/RITUALS FOR YOUR PERSONAL BOOK OF SHADOWS

Notes on Love Spells

Notes on Hexerei
Page - 61 -

Notes on Jinx Removing

Notes on Coven Affairs
Page - 66 -

BLESSED
BE

SPACE FOR YOUR NOTES/SPELLS/RITUALS FOR YOUR PERSONAL BOOK OF SHADOWS

Traditional Pennsylvania Dutch Hex Signs to draw Love and Friendship.

Paint them on the outside of the dwelling on a Day of Venus as the Moon waxes in a Water or an Earth Sign.

Paint them in shades of blue, red and yellow.

SPACE FOR YOUR NOTES/SPELLS/RITUALS FOR YOUR PERSONAL BOOK OF SHADOWS

STUDY WITH A TRUE MASTER OF THE ESOTERIC SCIENCES AND CHRISTIAN MYSTICISM

William Alexander Oribello

ADVANCED TEACHINGS TO BRING ABOUT ENLIGHTENMENT, INSPIRATION AND PROSPERITY AS HANDED DOWN FROM HIGHER REALMS AND OTHER DIMENSIONS

The following teachings by William Alexander Oribello are meant for the serious student who is seeking to discover new avenues of thinking and prosperity for individual and global enrichment.

❑ SACRED MAGIC Contains the essence of the mystic teachings given by the Magi and Masters of Wisdom to Wm Oribello. Here are: • 7 Great Money Secrets • Power In Spoken Words • The Key To Nature's Secrets • Individual Lucky Numbers • The Hidden Meaning of Stones, Colors and Candles. Oribello teaches how to develop psychic powers in a safe and powerful manner through methods that have not been shared since the Old Testament. Includes a series of talismans that originated with King Solomon, as well as a miniature replica of the Staff of Moses which is said to be the most powerful symbol given to humankind by God. This is the large size edition of the very potent teachings. - $17.50

❑ SEALED MAGICAL BOOK OF MOSES It is said that the Magical Art of Moses originally was told to select angels by none other than God. Later, when the race now called humans were expelled from the Garden of Eden, the angels taught this wisdom to humankind as a means for the race to find its way back to perfection. According to Oribello, "Moses possessed the wisdom to communicate with nature's finer forces in a manner known as miracles by the uninitiated. Here are the 12 MAGICAL TALISMANS OF MOSES seldom seen, which can be used to • Bring you to the highest possible good fortune • The blessings of being loved and have power over enemies • Help overcome illness and stay healthy • Make you a winner in games of chance • Bring loved ones back • Attain honor and personal wealth. - $17.50

❑ GODSPELLS-WRITTEN SPELLS, SPOKEN SPELLS AND ENHANCERS Wm Oribello teaches that even the word "Gospel" is taken from the ancient words meaning "God Spell," which is the concept this magical test is based upon. In a precise manner, the author tells the reader to perform over 50 Godspells, including • The Complete Rite of the magical word ABRACADABRA • Most powerful beauty spell • Spell to conquer fear • To overcome wicked people and situations • Good fortune. Additionally, Oribello provides the legendary power squares which have been handed down throughout the centuries only in sacred volumes until this time. There are Power Squares for • Business • Binding Enemies • Love • Youthfulness • Increased Intelligence. - $17.50

❑ CANDLE BURNING TO CONTACT YOUR GUARDIAN ANGEL Discover the "Seven Ministering Angels of the Seven Blessings," and how to connect with them to manifest the Seven Great Blessings in life, which are • Inner Power • Love • Prosperity • Mental Expansion • Psychic Awareness • Radiant Health • Cosmic Consciousness. Learn which colored candles to burn to contact the various types of angels; which planets govern which particular archangels; which specific day is ruled by each angel; how to become a "human angel." - $20.00

❑ CANDLE BURNING MAGIC WITH THE PSALMS Create life's greatest blessings by combining the power of the Holy Scriptures with the magic of burning different colored candles. The book's first section reveals the art of preparing candles to attract desired conditions and to repel unwanted conditions. The second section reveals an unusual technique to evoke the power of the Divine names, associated with the magical power of the Book of Psalms. The third section reveals the purpose for each of the Psalms and how to use them with these unique methods. Here are over 150 spells that repel evil or restless spirits. Overcome fear and persecution, and so much more. - $15.00

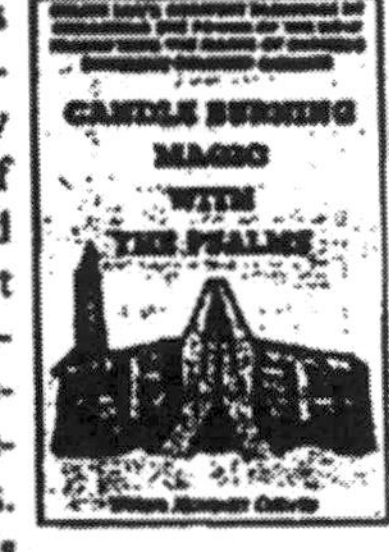

❑ MASTER BOOK OF SPIRITUAL POWER

Readers will learn of mysteries too sacred to be revealed to any but the highest of mystical initiates. Words and sounds so powerful that they can transcend time and space to attract the Lord's goodness without hesitance. These words are now yours to utter! You will be taught how to take ordinary items and transform them into powerful psychic tools to see the future. You will be instructed how to make an "Astral Tube" to see through walls and peer into other dimensions. Here is a 12-day program to rid yourself of all negativity and attract positive influences. - $17.50

❑ THE FINAL SOLUTION: CONTACT WITH THE MASTERS OF UNIVERSAL WISDOM-Much of the material in this work was channeled a number of years ago but its high vibrations can still be felt. Accurate illustrations on what the various Masters appear as when in physical form, and what they have individual command over so that you can draw them into your life. Other teachings of great benefit included in a work kept in print because so many have requested it after hearing how it has helped so many others. - $17.50

❑ COUNT ST. GERMAIN: THE PROPHET WHO LIVES FOREVER-Here is the history of the man who is almost 500 years old and has spoken with kings, queens and other world leaders over the centuries, and who could turn base metal into gold with his powers of alchemy. True health and metaphysical secrets that will make you look and feel younger. Includes conversations and channeling by Saint Germain (also see Oribello's video where he does actual channeling of the spiritual master). - $22.95 *(For complete Immortality Formula and Kit by Oribello, includes $30.00 extra).*

BE GUIDED AS YOU TRAVEL THROUGH LIFE TO FIND YOUR TRUE DESTINY

Facts About William Alexander Oribello

Since the 1960s, William Oribello has taught people from all walks of life how to improve themselves in all respects through the practical application of the mystic sciences as well as Christian Esotericism. Visits from angelic beings and Ascended Masters led to a lengthy and complete study of what Mr. Oribello defined as Sacred Magick or the Christ Mysteries. He understood that there was a deeper, hidden meaning to scripture which only serious students could understand. His best endeavor, ***Count St. Germain: The Prophet Who Lives Forever***, is preserved in print by Inner Light Publications. To disseminate Oribello's books more widely, Inner Light is offering a number of difficult to find books and video tapes. Learn the hidden meanings of existence to attain power over your life!

HIS LEGACY LIVES ON
WILLIAM ALEXANDER ORIBELLO
Master of Spiritism and the Mystic Sciences Wants You to Feel the Healing Powers of His

GALACTIC MASTERS & SPIRITUAL GUIDES

$42 A TRANSFORMATIONAL STUDY COURSE ON CD*
Complete With How-To Guides
*** Also Available on Cassette Tape**

Since the 1960s William Alexander Oribello has taught people, from all walks of life, how to improve themselves in every respect through the practical application of the mystic sciences. A visit at an early age from angelic beings (plus meetings with those whom he identified as the Masters of Universal Wisdom) led to a long understanding of Sacred Magic based on Old and New Testament Scriptures, which has continued to touch the lives of many through his books, tapes and study courses, despite his unfortunate passing a few years ago. His work is continued on an exclusive basis by his long time publisher, Inner Light.

❑ ORIBELLO'S SACRED MAGIC HEALING KIT

Along with his Cosmic Healing CD (or tape) you will receive a copy of Oribello's Sacred Magic, containing spiritual truths that will free you from pain, as well as tested techniques that can be applied by anyone wishing to improve their lives. The package also contains Oribello's previously unreleased 36 Techniques To Cosmic Understanding. In these important works the author reveals:

- The illusion that causes human suffering and the way out of the illusion.
- Techniques by which a practitioner may prepare for High Guidance.
- Ways in which you may develop your own inner potential in a safe and powerful manner by unlocking the secrets of nature.
- Know and apply the hidden secrets to be found within colors, stones and candles, as well as the power of the spoken word.
- You will also learn how to use a "magic" mirror* to look into your soul as well as how to find your individual lucky numbers to win at games of chance and bring you all you desire.

The principles Rev. Oribello teaches is not of the devil, but are based entirely upon God's words as handed down by the true Masters of all time.

COMPLETE HEALING PRACTITIONER'S KIT

Simply send $42.00 and we will also include FREE by William Alexander Oribello, the monographs, Personality Unmasked, (know what others are really like), and Inner Reflections which will reveal to you proof of God's existence and the best ways to discover true magic.

❑ **If you would like your own magic mirror, please add $40.00.**

MAGICKAL VIEWING

VIDEOS FOR ENLIGHTENMENT

RECENTLY DISCOVERED! HOW YOU CAN STUDY WITH WILLIAM ALEXANDER ORIBELLO IN YOUR OWN HOME!

❑ GET RICH QUICK SPELLS with William Alexander Oribello. Since the 1960s, Oribello has taught people from all walks of life how to improve themselves through the practical application of the Mystic Sciences. He is the author of such popular works as *Candle Burning With the Psalms; Sacred Magic* and *Godspells*. Taped at the New York Occult Center, this is a *hands on* presentation on the use of candles, herbs and oils to gain financial security and eliminate debt from your life. ***90 minutes.$21.95***

❑ VHS or ❑ DVD

❑ FIVE EASY STEPS TO PSYCHIC SELF DEFENSE with Wm Oribello. Is your life filled with negativity? Do you feel as if something "bad" is always going to happen? Has someone put the "evil eye" on you? If you feel down and out, this presentation will help remove these conditions and make you feel upbeat once again. Available now! ***Approximately 80 minutes $21.95***

❑ VHS or ❑ DVD

❑ SECRET SIGNS AND INVOCATIONS TO CONTACT ST. GERMAIN AND OTHER ASCENDED MASTERS. Taped under the influence of the violet ray at a Philadelphia workshop, William Oribello discusses his extensive career as a medium and a channel to the higher planes, and his ongoing contact with the Great White Brotherhood and other beings from various spiritual dimensions. Includes a dramatic channeling session and How-To inspirational information. ***Approximately 80 minutes. $21.95*** ❑ VHS or ❑ DVD

❑ **PURCHASE ALL THREE FOR ONLY $59.95 + $5.00 S/H**

HOW TO ORDER ITEMS ON THIS PAGE

Check desired items, clip pages and circle or use the handy order form on inside back cover. Add $5.00 S/H for up to 3 items; $6 for 4 or 5 items; $8 for 6 to 8 items; $10 for 9 or more items. All foreign *double the shipping* fees (some countries may be more). Use your VISA, MasterCard or Discover credit card and call our 24-hour automated hotline at 732-602-3407. Speak clearly and give all information. By mail from:

INNER LIGHT/GLOBAL COMMUNICATIONS
Box 753 • New Brunswick, NJ 08903
Please allow adequate time for delivery. NO CASH PLEASE.

23816634R00070

Made in the USA
Charleston, SC
03 November 2013